Learn to Cook

25

Southern Classics

3 Ways

Learn to Cook

25

Southern Classics

3 Ways

Traditional, Contemporary, International

Jennifer Brulé

The University of North Carolina Press   CHAPEL HILL

Text © 2016 The University of North Carolina Press
Photographs © 2016 Jennifer Brulé
Line drawings © 2016 Jill Seale
Sunbursts © 2016 Stella's Graphic Supply / Creative Market
All rights reserved
Manufactured in the United States of America
Designed by Kimberly Bryant and set in Merlo by Rebecca Evans

The University of North Carolina Press has been a member of
the Green Press Initiative since 2003.

Cover illustrations: background, istockphoto.com / hanohiki; line drawings © Jill Seale,
www.jillseale.com; sunburst © Stella's Graphic Supply / Creative Market

Library of Congress Cataloging-in-Publication Data
Names: Brulé, Jennifer, author.
Title: Learn to cook 25 Southern classics 3 ways : traditional, contemporary, international /
    Jennifer Brulé.
Other titles: Learn to cook twenty-five Southern classics three ways
Description: Chapel Hill : The University of North Carolina Press, [2016] | Includes index.
Identifiers: LCCN 2016012031| ISBN 9781469629124 (cloth : alk. paper) | ISBN 9781469629131
    (ebook)
Subjects: LCSH: Cooking, American—Southern style. | International cooking. |
    LCGFT: Cookbooks.
Classification: LCC TX715.2.S68 B789 2016 | DDC 641.5975—dc23 LC record available at
    http://lccn.loc.gov/2016012031

Contents

Picnic spread. Photograph by Monica Galloway.

Preface

I lied to my mother. I lied because of an overwhelming desire for Velveeta cheese. It was 1980 and I was a twelve-year-old latch-key kid: That is, I walked home from school and opened the door to my house using a key that hung on a piece of red-and-white butcher's twine around my neck. Alone in the house, I'd make a snack and watch TV until my parents got home from work. This was rather common in those days in families where both parents worked.

But this morning I had indirectly lied to my mother. The rule was that once I was home, I stayed there, inside the house. This afternoon I planned to leave the house, walk the half mile down the street to the Big Bear grocery store, and buy a brick of Velveeta cheese. My mother would have had two problems with this scenario: (1) I left the house and walked to the grocery store, which entailed crossing a very busy five-lane street, and (2) I bought a brick of Velveeta cheese.

The week before, I had tasted Velveeta for the first time at my friend Lara's house. Her mother made me a grilled cheese sandwich with it, and the gooey, salty goodness blew my mind. Both my parents were exceptional cooks. Grilled cheese sandwiches at my house were a rarity, but when they did make an appearance, they were crafted strictly from sharp British cheddar, or possibly a French Camembert, never from processed cheese. That curiously slurpable Velveeta grilled cheese made my head spin.

My corduroys made a *zip-zip-zip* sound as I speed-walked toward the grocery store. A few tentative, staccato jumps across the busy street landed me in the market's parking lot. It took me a while to find the Velveeta in the store. Because it was called "cheese," I made the incorrect assumption it would be in the refrigerated cheese case. I finally found it high up on a shelf near the bread. I stood in line waiting to pay for my heavy brick of "processed cheese food" feeling sneaky and scared and nervous and defiant.

Back across the busy street, I was more emboldened now, carrying the yellow rectangular box like a hard-won prize. I arrived home and immediately began microwaving thick gelatinous slices one after another, eating the golden, molten cheese-lava with a spoon. I ate half of the brick (which is about the weight of a toddler) and threw the remaining half, the evidence, in the trash.

Although I skipped dinner that night, complaining (quite honestly) of a stomachache, my mother never found out that I had walked to the grocery store and tainted her brand-new microwave with processed cheese.

My life has been delineated by memorable food moments, from gourmet to greasy spoon. Food, cooking, and family are what make up my life experiences, and they always intertwine. After the birth of my first baby, I was most excited about her first meal. I imagined it and planned it for eight months, until she was old enough to eat table food. I made her risotto with smoked salmon and squished sweet peas. She loved it. She took the spoon from me and ate the rest of the sticky rice with her hands. I don't remember her first steps, but I will never forget her first meal.

If I am not cooking, I'm distracted by thoughts of cooking. It is my singular obsession. I'm not stating that to be boastful—I'm not even sure that it's a good thing to have such a one-track mind. It's just how I am wired.

For me, attention to food and cooking are like unchecked compulsions. Thankfully, there is a special school for people like me—it's called culinary school. It was there that I learned the crucial and proper cooking techniques, but it has been the five to eight hours of cooking each day (over the last twenty-one years) that have refined my art. To me, cooking truly is an artistic expression of love.

I've been lucky that magazine editors and television producers see the value in my art. I've cobbled together a tremendously fulfilling career in food writing and food television. I've developed recipes for national magazines and popular mommy-blogs and appeared in countless cooking segments on North Carolina television stations. I've also had the great fortune to teach cooking to children, teens, and adults in three different countries, to dozens of different nationalities—always learning as much about food from my students as they learned about cooking from me.

One thing I know for sure is that most people like to eat. A handful of people have told me that they would rather take a pill than eat a meal. Part of me, about thirty pounds of me, wishes that I had a bit of that apathy toward eating, but mostly I am confused by that sentiment. For me, cooking and eating are about so much more than sustenance.

What led me to write a cookbook about southern cooking, and to use these iconic dishes as a way to teach cooking techniques, was my career as a food writer and cooking teacher and the years my family spent living in both the American South and Europe.

About twelve years ago, our family was living in Augusta, Georgia, and I was a food writer for the *Augusta Chronicle*—and then my husband's company moved us to Switzerland. The expat adventure that we thought would last just two years ended up stretching into seven years and two countries.

From our home base in Zürich, our family traveled every possible chance we had. I would drive forty-five minutes into Germany to grocery shop, or I'd join a friend for the ninety-minute drive to France for lunch, just because I could. Later, when we lived in northwestern England, our family spent sunny weekends seeking out windy beaches in Wales, squishing through soggy moors in England's Lake District, or making exciting, urban visits to Edinburgh, Scotland.

We crammed our family of six into our minivan and drove all over Europe on weekends and every school holiday, seeking out new places to explore and foods to eat. We packed the diaper bag and set off for a long weekend in Lyon, France, when our twins were just eight weeks out of the hospital.

Traveling became, and remains, our family's collective obsession. It didn't take me long to realize that no matter which part of the world we were in, what people cooked and ate would tell me a lot about their culture and what they held dear. And that's why I think it's so critical that we take an interest in what we are eating and feeding our families.

I grew up in Columbus, Ohio, in a comfortable but homogeneous suburb. Because the cost of taking a family of seven out to dinner was prohibitive, and because Columbus simply didn't have a great variety of restaurants in those days, we rarely ate out—maybe just a few times a year. Luckily, both of my parents adored cooking. Our kitchen was outfitted with stainless steel counters and restaurant equipment before that was a thing. It was actually a point of ridicule from friends who didn't understand why we would have an ugly black eight-burner gas stove in our kitchen rather than a sleek avocado-green electric one.

When I was sixteen, my parents indulged a lifelong dream and took off to spend the summer in Paris. There they absorbed the culture, took many cooking classes, and ate lingering lunches in fancy French restaurants. When they returned home, they went back to their regular jobs but began teaching cooking classes at night. At eighty-three years old today, they still teach cooking classes. They are definitely the reason I am a food writer and cooking teacher.

Although I am a classically trained chef, I attended culinary school in order to become a well-educated food writer and cooking teacher, not to work in a restaurant, although I've done a little of that, too. Teaching cooking classes lets me connect personally with other people who love food and are curious to learn more about cooking. Writing about food and making TV appearances helps me reach a broader audience to spread the gospel of good food.

A few years ago, my neighbor Sarah told me, "Your recipes convince me to cook things that I think I am going to hate . . . and then I end up loving them!" This was the best compliment I've ever received, because it's exactly what I try to do—surprise people by their appreciation for foods yet unknown to their palate and by their own ability to cook them.

And in that sense I'm no different than most people. I love trying something new—discovering obscure ingredients or dishes from random parts of the world and cooking them in my own kitchen. But of course there are days when I am just craving something familiar and comforting, like a steaming bowl of chicken and dumplings. Those meals are balanced by my awareness of healthy eating and the knowledge that preparing alternatives to the comfort foods doesn't mean relinquishing amazing flavors.

Acknowledgments

My intense, lifelong passion for food stems from growing up in a household where cooking was almost an intellectual endeavor. It was seen as an event to be discussed, deliberated, and often deconstructed; the process was generally as important as the resulting meal.

It made an impact on me that both of my parents, rather than just my mother, shared this passion (and still do). I grew up in the 1970s and '80s, when, for the most part, the only men interested in cooking were professional chefs, not suburban dads. Save for Sunday cookouts or fish fry-ups, most of my friends' fathers left the preparation of food up to their wives. That's just the way it was then. So the fact that my father would toil away in the kitchen, finding the best recipe for buckwheat crepes or chocolate layer cake, made cooking seem more of an interest, a passion, than a mandatory household task that women of that time typically would take care of.

In my teens, dinner conversations were made up mainly of talking about the ingredients and methods used in preparing the meal (how it could have been different with any slight alteration, or where the inspiration for the meal came from), spiked with news of local and world events.

Between the weird French food and the tedious table conversation, my friends didn't often stay for dinner.

I met my husband, Jeff, while I was attending culinary school in Baltimore and he was working at his first postcollege job. Jeff came from a very physically active family—always on the go, usually outdoors in a boat or playing sports. Food was not the center of their lives. Jeff was twenty-three when we met, and he had never eaten a salad (I'm not kidding). That changed as soon as we began dating, and over the past twenty-two years he has become an expert recipe taster. Because of his work around the world, he has also become an impressively fearless eater, consuming weird foods in far-off lands, dishes I wouldn't dream of eating.

Jeff and I have four compassionate, outspoken, hilarious daughters. They always stand up for the little guy and usually have a joke at the ready, and there are no people I'd rather spend time with. They are truly my best friends.

So I'd like to thank first and foremost those seven very influential people: my parents, Bill and Ginsie Ress; my husband, Jeff; and our daughters, Claire, Camille, Mimi, and Tess.

A huge thank-you to Elaine Maisner, my editor at UNC Press. Her no-nonsense guidance and advice helped me shape this book into what it is, a teaching cookbook. Special thanks to Mary Caviness at the Press for her patience.

Thanks also to three women whose creativity and patience are reflected throughout this book. Photographer Monica Galloway helped so much in editing my recipe photos. She also took the beautifully composed multi-food shots you'll see. She is a wonderful photographer and friend. My dear friend Jill Seale is the remarkable artist responsible for the sweet drawings you'll see scattered throughout this book. Linda Brulé, my mother-in-law, took on the monumental task of being a second pair of eyes, as she painstakingly read through every word of this book before I sent it off to UNC Press. I'm lucky to have such gifted and generous women in my life!

Last, I'd like to sincerely thank the friends who tested recipes for this cookbook. Some of them are superior home cooks, while others were just getting their kitchen legs beneath them. I found comments from both types of cooks invaluable—the expert cooks had fabulously detailed feedback, while the rookies brought up questions that my classically trained eye had overlooked. Jennifer Slosson, Laura Ashley Cherry, Kim Kusterer, Hunter Busse, Monica Galloway, Stacy Baker, Carly Schiano, Allison Powers, Jen Swart, Anne Arms, Heather Ward, Courtney Spear, Karol Cerosky, and Susanne Kondracke: Your unwavering enthusiasm and considerate comments were a tremendous source of inspiration and validation for me. Thank you!

Acknowledgments

Learn to Cook

25

Southern

Classics

3 Ways

Dinner buffet. Photograph by Monica Galloway.

Introduction

Early into our expat adventure in Switzerland, my family fell in love with Ticino, the country's Italian region. We drove the short two-and-a-half-hour crossing through the Alps to visit this area every chance we got. I first tasted Polenta e Gorgonzola at a sunny trattoria in Lugano. I quickly realized that Polenta e Gorgonzola was nothing more than Italian cheese grits—something I was very familiar with and adept at preparing when we'd lived in Georgia.

As I savored each bite, it occurred to me that the world of food was really quite small—that methods of cooking are frequently the same around the globe; it's the ingredients that change. As soon as that idea sank in, I began thinking of ways to teach very basic cooking techniques that would open up a world of cuisines to all kinds of cooks, from beginners to seasoned home chefs wanting to learn something new.

After many years and countless memories made in Europe, my family moved back to the United States, back to the South. Our oldest daughter, then in eighth grade, was the only one of our children who had ever gone to an American school, and just kindergarten at that. The other three had never been in an American school, and the twins had never even lived in the United States—they thought that America was strictly somewhere one went on vacation, because that was all they had ever done here. I was nervous about repatriation into our home country, because my children didn't think of the United States as home, per se. When we arrived in a little college town in North Carolina and settled in instantly, we were all tremendously relieved.

I soon found that I was acclimating to our new home in the South exactly as I had in other countries—through food. I sought out farmers' markets, small mom-and-pop country stores, and roadside seafood or vegetable stands. I tasted foods that I was unfamiliar with, asked questions, and absorbed answers.

Like Europe, the South is made up of innumerable regions, each with different customs, histories, and foods specific to that exact part of the world. Experiencing those regions through food brings texture to the geographic fabric. Learning about which foods are celebrated through festivals, or which dishes are saved only for special occasions, helps to color the regions in.

I've now lived nearly a decade in the South. While that may not make me a southerner, I am of the South.

I've learned that, in traditional southern foodways, vegetables often took center stage on many tables. As in many other countries in the world, meat was costly and often used more as a seasoning agent than the central feature. This tradition has stuck around. Southerners love their seasonal vegetables and long ago figured out how to turn the most bountiful garden dwellers into remarkable dishes.

In addition to the endless creative vegetable dishes that appear as the main attraction on the southern table, there are always plenty of comforting side dishes, too. No matter your religion, if you are lucky enough to attend a southern church picnic on Sunday, you will see the most amazing array of these side dishes (deviled eggs, pimento cheese sandwiches, ham biscuits, and artichoke relish, to name a few).

While vegetables and side dishes are the mainstay in the South, there are occasions when meat is more prominently featured. Many old-time southern families raised a pig or two as their main source of meat for the year and used up every bit of the critter (that's where livermush, pork rinds, and pickled pigs' feet come from). These foods aren't eaten as often as they used to be, but there is still a livermush festival every fall in Shelby, North Carolina (replete with a Little Miss Livermush pageant). I find comfort knowing that I can pick up a jar of pickled pigs' feet any-time I want at my local grocery store. I'm not joking about that. I call these culinary anomalies legacy foods. Every culture has them. The fact that many grocery stores in my area continue to carry legacy foods (like pickled pigs' feet)—not just run-of-the-mill, homogenized, factory-made foods—makes me sanguine about the southern food scene.

The culinary soul of the South has solid footing in a broad and deep diversity of peoples and regions. The long history alone is impressive—many recipes date back four hundred years. But it's the flood of vast and various cultures influencing the southern kitchen that I find most impressive. West African, French, Spanish, Mexican, British, Scottish, Native American, and others—each culture has had a hand in what we've come to know as classic southern recipes. Food is so obviously more than sustenance. It's our heritage—our past *and* our future.

Over the past twenty years, Americans have gained a more experimental and global palate, but often their practical ability to cook has not kept up. I think this is due in part to our ever-expanding culinary world (it's possible to gather ingredients from all over the world right in our local grocery store) and our awareness of it (thanks to cooking channels and YouTube videos) in combination with our busy lives. The act of cooking often comes in last even for people who love to eat well.

Sometimes, though, we do have time to spend preparing dinner and sitting down to enjoy it. On those evenings, I hope you will pull out this book and be inspired to cook. It could be on a whim or on a few designated nights each week, when schedules allow, or on the weekends when time seems more abundant.

My aim is to encourage you to cook whenever possible and enjoy not only the outcome but also the process. My hope is that this book will inspire you to cook and that you will come to love the act and the art of cooking.

Here's the craziest part of my culinary ethos: It's not hard.

It's not hard to cook authentic southern foods, just like it's not necessarily hard to cook fabulous French food, or Swiss, or Cuban, or Vietnamese. *Learn to Cook 25 Southern Classics 3 Ways* shows you exactly how to make the juiciest traditional southern fried chicken, and then it takes you a step further: It teaches you that, by using the same techniques and just a few ingredient changes, you can successfully make a contemporary, lighter version—Crispy Oven-Fried Chicken—and then, by using a different cut of chicken but the same baking method, you can make an internationally inspired version, Spicy Baked Piri Piri Wings. Each set of recipes (classic, contemporary, and international) will reinforce either cooking methods (sautéing or pan-frying, for example), a skill (say, knife skills or whipping egg whites), or ingredients (cornmeal or cube steak, for instance), and sometimes all three. Repetition is key to learning.

The "contemporary" recipes in this book offer a healthier take on the classics: A recipe may replace animal-based fats (like butter) with plant-based fats (like coconut oil), or add nutritionally dense ingredients to a recipe, rather than taking an ingredient away. In any case, the most important element of every contemporary recipe is fantastic flavor. Purists take note: The "international" recipes are not replicas of global recipes; rather, they take inspiration from countries and regions around the world. They are not authentic renditions of international dishes, but my riff on foreign dishes.

I aim to show you how to learn classic southern cooking—and two twists. Three dishes in a flash.

Cooking Terms

Bake: To cook in the oven, covered or uncovered, using dry heat. Cookies, pies, cakes, and breads all use the baking method. *Note:* All of the recipes in this book were developed and tested in ovens that did not use a convection fan. If your oven has a convection option, baking and roasting temperatures may need to be adjusted, 10–20 percent lower, but please refer to the oven's manual to double check.

Beat: To mix vigorously, incorporating air, until mixture is smooth.

Boil: To heat liquid until bubbles consistently and rapidly break at the surface. Most often used in cooking potatoes and pasta.

Braise: To cook food such as a tough cut of meat slowly over moist heat: in a tightly covered pan, either on top of the stove or in the oven, in a small amount of liquid.

Chop: To cut solid foods into small pieces.

Cream: A baking term used when beating together solid fat, like butter, shortening, lard, or coconut oil, with sugar. The two are beaten together until well combined and lighter in both density and usually color.

Deglaze: To add liquid to a pan that has cooked-on bits of food and fat, called fond. The liquid dissolves the cooked-on pieces and absorbs their flavor.

Dimple: When heating oil to sauté or shallow fry, this is the term used to describe the appearance of the oil's surface: small indentations in the oil that look like the dimples in a smiling face.

Dock: To prick small holes in dough (piecrust, for example) to allow steam to evenly escape as the dough bakes.

Dredge: To coat food, like raw chicken or fish pieces, in a dry ingredient like flour, cornstarch, cornmeal, or bread crumbs, before cooking to create a crust.

Drizzle: To pour a thin stream of liquid onto food (like oil over salad greens).

Fold: To gently mix ingredients together without decreasing volume, usually from incorporated air bubbles.

Grate: To rub a food, such as a piece of hard cheese, a carrot, or a whole nutmeg, across a grater to shred the food into small pieces.

Knead: To press dough using the heels of your hands, folding and pressing until dough is smooth. This develops the gluten in flour-based doughs.

Macerate: To soften (usually fruits or vegetables) by soaking in liquid, sometimes the ingredients' own juices. For example, fruits in cobbler release their own juices when sugar is added.

Mince: To chop solid foods into very fine pieces.

Poach: To gently cook food, such as an egg or a piece of fish, in very hot but not boiling liquid.

Preheat: To heat up an oven or pan, usually to a specific temperature, before beginning to cook.

Sauté: To cook food in a sauté pan or skillet in a very small amount of fat at a relatively high heat.

Shallow fry: To cook food that is only partially covered with oil, not fully submerged (as in deep frying). Because food is only partially covered in oil, it must be turned over during frying to cook both sides.

Simmer: To cook food submerged in hot liquid, just below the boiling point, where consistent but gentle bubbles rise to the surface.

Steam: To cook food in the hot vapor that rises from boiling or simmering liquid. The food should not touch the hot liquid.

Whisk: To stir, beat, or whip with a wire whisk or fork in order to combine ingredients and incorporate air.

Umami: The fifth taste (in addition to sweet, sour, salty, and bitter). It's a depth of flavor, a richness or savoriness (but not necessarily salty). Food rich in umami: aged or fermented foods (like Parmigiano-Reggiano cheese, fish sauce, soy sauce, or Marmite), sun-dried tomatoes, seaweed, and cured or roasted meats.

Zest: The colored part of the skin of a citrus fruit—the part that holds the essential oils (the flavor and fragrance). Adding citrus zest to salad dressings, sauces, marinades, rubs, olive oil, or butter adds the essence of that citrus fruit. Make sure not to use the white part that's just beneath the zest (this is called pith), as it's bitter.

Essential Kitchen Equipment

Box grater: A very useful, old-school, four-sided gadget that shreds cheese, zests citrus, grinds fresh nutmeg, minces garlic, slices cucumber, and much more. It has numerous uses and is inexpensive—a must-have.

Candy thermometer: A large thermometer that registers heat between 100° and 400°. Used to measure the temperature of cooked sugar at different stages and to measure the temperature of fat for frying.

Cast-iron skillet: Traditional yet more popular than ever for chefs as well as home cooks, cast-iron cookware is almost indestructible. Don't leave high-acid foods, such as tomatoes, in cast-iron pans for long, however, as the acid in the tomatoes can harm the cast iron.

Dutch oven: A large, heavy pot with a tight-fitting lid. Usually but not exclusively made of cast iron.

Immersion blender: A hand-held electric appliance that can be submerged into wet food such as soups, sauces, or dressings to blend and purée. It's an invaluable, affordable kitchen tool.

Instant-read thermometer: A small thermometer with a sharp metal probe that is inserted into cooked foods (usually meats) to take the internal temperature. Found in cooking supply stores and in many supermarkets.

Jelly roll pan: A sheet pan with 1-inch-high sides. Great at holding liquids in during roasting.

Microplane: Brand name used interchangeably for a multiuse gadget that serves as a citrus zester, hard cheese grater, chocolate grater, even a fresh truffle grater. It's inexpensive and can replace many other gadgets.

Silpat: Brand name used interchangeably for a silicone, nonstick, reusable baking mat. Very useful in the kitchen.

Wire whisk: A utensil used to whip wet ingredients and/or incorporate air, as in egg whites or whipped cream. The most common is the teardrop shape, called a balloon whisk.

Pantry Secrets

This is my own take on a few special ingredients that will make what you cook taste even better.

Coconut oil: Although coconut oil is a saturated fat, it doesn't contain cholesterol. It has a high smoke point, which means it's great for using to sauté, when the heat is blasting. Coconut oil leaves zero coconut flavor. It comes solid, usually in a jar, and melts when even slightly warmed.

Cream of tartar: Potassium hydrogen tartrate, an acid that reacts with the egg whites, making them more stable when whipped.

Extra-virgin olive oil: Look for the words "cold pressed" on the label, which indicates that heat was not applied when the oil was extracted from the olives, which can destroy the oil's delicate flavor. Best used to finish dishes or make excellent salad dressings. Drizzle fruity olive oil over cooked lentils or pasta with a squeeze of lemon juice and a scattering of sea salt, and you've got dinner.

Fish sauce: Think fish sauce is just for Southeast Asian recipes? Nope—it adds umami—a Japanese word for a deep, rich taste— that is unparalleled in the condiment world. Use fish sauce in marinades for beef, in soups, in baked beans, even in guacamole. You will not detect it as a "fishy" taste, and your food will just be slightly more delicious. Hold your nose and use it!

Garlic powder and onion powder: Adding garlic powder and/or onion powder to a seasoning mix for grilled, fried, or roasted meat and fish gives a little oomph to the finished dish. Make sure to buy garlic or onion powder, not garlic or onion salt. Season as you like, adding your own salt as needed.

Kosher or sea salt flakes: Kosher and sea salts usually don't contain the iodine that table salt does. They have a cleaner flavor, without the metallic notes that table salt can have. Kosher salt flakes are too big to flow from a salt shaker and need to be scattered over food by hand.

Nonstick cooking spray: Useful for so many applications, nonstick cooking spray adds little to no fat and just makes life easier.

Parmigiano-Reggiano cheese: When a recipe calls for Parmesan cheese, this is the best one to use. It's expensive, yes—but a little goes a long way, and the flavor is incomparable to cheaper versions. Buy only the amount you need, and grate it only when you need it. The deep, almost fruity notes of this Italian beauty can turn up the flavor factor in every dish in which it's used.

Peanut oil: Traditionally used for frying in the South, partly because that's where peanuts are grown and partly because it's got a high smoke point. It's a good all-purpose oil. If you can't use peanut oil, canola oil is a good substitute.

Peppercorns cracked in a pepper mill: Freshly cracked pepper tastes entirely different from the preground pepper in a tin box; its flavor and spiciness is far more intense. It's well worth investing in a pepper mill, even one of those disposable ones found in the grocer's spice aisle.

Popcorn salt: Popcorn salt is much finer than table, sea, or kosher salt. It clings to foods, especially fried foods, really well. Popcorn salt is made not for cooking, but for finishing: for seasoning up fried green tomatoes, oven-baked sweet potato fries, and crunchy fried fish as soon as they come out of the pan.

Sambal oelek: Whereas sriracha is used as a condiment for finished dishes, sambal oelek is a chili paste used during cooking to add the same spicy goodness. It's chunkier and funkier than sriracha and is a great addition to marinades, soups, or stews.

Smoked paprika: Made of dried, smoked, and pulverized *Capsicum annuum* peppers, a little of this adds a rich background note, and more adds a wonderful, smoky essence. I use smoked paprika in a surprising number of recipes; with a light hand, it gives an added layer of deliciousness that is undefinable.

Soy sauce: Look for "brewed" written on the label. Cheap brands pass off salty, brown liquid as soy sauce, but high-quality soy sauce is brewed (like the easily found Kikkoman's). It adds more than salt—it lends a depth of flavor.

Sriracha: A hot trend in condiments, Thailand's sriracha sauce is a smooth, spicy condiment made from chili peppers, garlic, and other spices. It's to be used after cooking, giving dishes a wonderfully, spicy kick.

Truffle salt: People either love truffle salt or hate it. I am addicted, but my husband won't even sit at the table if I am using it. If you can, taste truffle salt before investing in a costly jar and buy the smallest quantity possible. The truffle salt most people are familiar with is predominantly flavored with synthetic truffle "aroma." Natural truffles are fragile; they lose their flavor and fragrance quickly. So while the ingredients list on the bottle may read "truffle," it will most likely also read "truffle aroma," which indicates a man-made product. This isn't necessarily a bad thing; it's still delicious, it's just not what real truffles taste like!

1

Classic Southern Fried Chicken

CONTEMPORARY **CRISPY OVEN-FRIED CHICKEN**

INTERNATIONAL **SPICY BAKED PIRI PIRI WINGS**

The crisp crunch of a piece of homemade fried chicken is a rare treat. For many people, frying chicken at home is intimidating because it requires extra effort, but that effort is absolutely worth it! Homemade fried chicken just can't be matched in flavor or crunch appeal by fast-food or store-bought fried chicken. The most important asset one can have in making outstanding fried chicken at home is simply, attention. Keeping the oil temperature constant is the most important factor, and this requires constant attention—there's no turning your back on frying chicken. Like pork chops, frying bone-in chicken pieces will add depth and flavor to the finished dish.

In the Crispy Oven-Fried Chicken, you'll use the same pieces of chicken as in the classic recipe and the same method of marinating in buttermilk but then depart from the classic version by baking them in the oven. They turn out crisp, flavorful, and ready to be the star of any meal.

Finally, no chicken section would be complete without the inclusion of chicken wings. Once used mainly for making stock, they have become stratospherically popular in restaurants—and ridiculously easy to bake up in the oven at home. I'll share with you a secret cooking tip to make the wings bake up incredibly crisp, and you'll reinforce those baking skills learned in the oven-baked fried chicken recipe.

Classic Southern Fried Chicken

Makes 4–6 servings

If there is one recipe widely associated with the South, it may be fried chicken. Delicious in its simplicity—nothing more than a farm-fresh chicken, buttermilk, a splash of hot sauce, and flour. Make sure to give yourself ample time when frying chicken. It's not a quick dish: Like any good relationship, it requires time and attention.

Fried chicken transcends any socioeconomic framework. Home-made fried chicken is in a class by itself.

> 1 chicken (about 3 pounds), cut into 8 pieces
>   (breasts cut in half, widthwise)
> 2 cups buttermilk
> 2 teaspoons hot sauce
> 2–3 cups peanut oil
> 2 cups all-purpose flour
> 1 tablespoon seasoned salt (like Lawry's brand)

If you don't have a candy thermometer, you can determine whether oil is hot enough for frying the old-school way: Heat the oil, covered, over medium heat for about 5–7 minutes, then flick a few drops of water into it. If the water makes the oil bubble steadily, it's ready for frying; if it crackles wildly, it's too hot and the heat needs to be lowered; and if it doesn't bubble at all, it's not hot enough yet.

You can find whole chickens cut up in most grocery store meat sections.

1 Place the chicken in a 1-gallon zip-top plastic bag and pour in the buttermilk and hot sauce. Zip the top shut and turn the chicken so that the marinade coats every piece. Place the bag in a large bowl and refrigerate. Marinate at least 2 hours (but no longer than 4, or the lactic acid in the milk that tenderizes the chicken could make the meat tough).

2 Remove the chicken from the refrigerator 30 minutes before frying. Pour the peanut oil into a 10- or 12-inch cast-iron skillet or
   heavy sauté pan. The oil should come about 1–2 inches up the
   inside of the skillet—this is called shallow frying. Be sure that the
   oil is at least 2 inches below the top of the pan; otherwise it could
   spill over once you put the chicken in. Cover and set over medium
   heat until it reaches 325–350° (use a candy thermometer, but if you
   don't have one, see the instructions above on how to know if the
   oil is hot enough for frying).

3 Meanwhile, toss the flour and seasoned salt together in a large
   bowl. One at a time, remove the chicken pieces from the buttermilk, allowing excess buttermilk to drain off. Place a piece of the
   chicken in the bowl of flour and toss to coat entirely (this is called
   dredging), then place the dredged chicken on a wire rack skin-side
   up and continue dredging the rest of the chicken.

4 Preheat the oven to 200°. Fit a jelly roll pan with a wire rack.

5 When the oil is 325–350°, carefully lay the breaded chicken
   pieces in the skillet—a 12-inch skillet can comfortably hold three
   drumsticks or two large thighs or one large breast cut in half.
   The chicken needs plenty of room to fry properly, but it should
   not be submerged in oil: There should be 1–2 inches of oil around
   each piece, and the oil should come halfway up the side of each
   piece. Cover the skillet, with just the tiniest crack between the lid
   and the skillet to allow some steam to escape. Set a timer and fry
   for 10 minutes. Here is where you must watch the oil temperature
   and possibly adjust the heat slightly—the temperature needs to
   remain between 325° and 350°, with bubbles breaking around the
   chicken consistently but not vigorously.

6 After 10 minutes of frying, use tongs to turn the chicken pieces
   over, set the timer again for 12 minutes and fry, *uncovered* now.
   Carefully watch the oil temperature; it needs to remain at
   325–350°.

7 Remove the chicken from the skillet and place it on the prepared
   pan. The chicken's internal temperature, taken with an instant-
   read thermometer, should be 165–170°. Set the tray of chicken in
   the oven. Keep all of the chicken there as you fry, to keep it warm.

Crispy Oven-Fried Chicken

Makes 6 servings

Surprisingly crunchy, flavorful, and healthy. This is a great alternative to traditional southern fried chicken.

1 chicken (about 3 pounds), cut into 8 pieces
    (breasts cut in half, widthwise)
3 cups buttermilk, divided
2 teaspoons hot sauce
1 cup all-purpose flour
1 cup cornstarch
4 eggs
1½ cups crushed Ritz crackers (about 36 crackers)
1 cup panko bread crumbs
1 teaspoon onion powder
½ teaspoon garlic powder
½–1 teaspoon seasoned salt (like Lawry's brand)
2 teaspoons poultry seasoning, or 1 teaspoon dried thyme
    and 1 teaspoon dried sage
½ teaspoon smoked paprika
½ cup plus 2 tablespoons melted coconut oil

HOW TO BREAD WITHOUT BREADING YOUR HANDS

Make sure your breading station (3 separate pie plates or bowls for the flour/corn-meal, egg wash, and bread crumb mixture) are set up before beginning. Designate one hand to be the "wet" hand and the other to be the "dry" hand. The wet hand removes the chicken from the buttermilk, places it on the paper towels to blot off the excess buttermilk, then places it into the flour/cornmeal. The dry hand covers the chicken in the flour/cornmeal and transfers it to the egg wash. The wet hand takes over again here, making sure that the chicken is covered in egg wash, then transferring it to the bread crumb mixture, where the dry hand again takes over, coating the chicken in bread crumbs and finally moving the chicken to the wire rack.

1 Place the chicken in a 1-gallon zip-top plastic bag and pour in 2 cups of the buttermilk and the hot sauce. Zip the top shut and turn the chicken so that the marinade coats every piece. Place the bag in a large bowl and then put the bowl in the refrigerator. Marinate for 2–4 hours (but no longer than that, or the lactic acid in the milk could make the meat tough).

2 Preheat the oven to 350°. Set up the breading station: In a pie plate, mix the flour and cornstarch together. In a second pie plate, whisk together the eggs and the remaining buttermilk with a fork until uniformly yellow. In a third pie plate, combine the cracker crumbs, bread crumbs, onion powder, garlic powder, seasoned salt, poultry seasoning (or dried herbs), and paprika. Place several layers of paper towels on dinner plates.

3 Remove the chicken from the refrigerator and, one piece at time, remove it from the buttermilk, allowing excess buttermilk to drain back into the plastic bag or the sink. Place the chicken pieces onto the paper towels and blot them to soak up excess liquid. Discard the buttermilk and paper towels.

Crispy Oven-Fried Chicken

4 Spray a large sheet pan with nonstick cooking spray. Working with one piece at a time, dredge the chicken in flour, making sure that it's completely covered—shake any excess back into the bowl. Next place it into the bowl of egg/buttermilk and turn to coat evenly. Finally, place the gooey chicken piece into the bowl of cracker crumbs, turning and patting the crumbs onto the chicken to coat well. Place the finished chicken pieces onto the prepared pan and continue to bread the remaining pieces.

5 When all the chicken pieces have been breaded, drizzle ½ teaspoon of the coconut oil evenly on each side of the chicken and rub it in with the back of a spoon to spread it evenly across the breading. Bake for 30 minutes, remove from the oven, and spread ½ teaspoon of coconut oil on the side of the chicken facing up, then flip it over. Return the chicken to the oven and bake for 25–30 minutes longer. When the chicken is done, the internal temperature should be 165–170°.

Spicy Baked Piri Piri Wings

Piri Piri sauce is Portuguese by way of Mozambique. The Piri Piri pepper is an African bird's-eye chili pepper that is very hot, and also very hard to find in American grocery stores, so I've replaced them in this recipe with Fresno, jalapeño, or serrano peppers (whichever of these you can most easily find). While this sauce has a spicy kick (it's about as spicy as hot buffalo sauce), its heat doesn't overtake the other vibrant flavors. The addition of brown sugar and fish sauce is completely inauthentic, but neither ingredient is pronounced and together they round out the flavor profile nicely.

Makes approximately 6 servings

FOR THE SAUCE

2 tablespoons light olive oil, vegetable oil, or coconut oil

3 fat garlic cloves, roughly chopped

½ medium yellow onion, peeled and roughly chopped

4 Fresno peppers (jalapeño or serrano peppers can be substituted), stem, membranes, and seeds removed, peppers roughly chopped

1 roasted red pepper (from a jar is fine), roughly chopped

Juice of 1 lemon

1 teaspoon apple cider vinegar

3 teaspoons lightly packed light brown sugar

3 tablespoons water

1 teaspoon kosher or sea salt

1 teaspoon fish sauce

FOR THE WINGS

3½ pounds chicken wings

1 tablespoon baking powder

1 teaspoon kosher or sea salt

A FEW SIMPLE TRICKS TO MAKING CRISPY BAKED WINGS

1 Make sure that the wings are completely dry before beginning.

2 Use baking powder to create a delicate, crunchy crust.

3 Don't crowd the baking sheet; make sure that each wing has at least half an inch around it so that air can circulate. If the wings are too close, they will steam rather than dry roast. This is an excellent method for making any type of oven-baked wings.

4 Toss the wings with your choice of sauce immediately after they come out of the oven and serve hot.

1. For the sauce: Heat the oil in a small pot or pan over medium heat. When the oil starts to dimple, add the garlic, onions, Fresno peppers, and roasted red peppers and stir well. Raise the heat to medium-high and sauté, stirring often, until the peppers begin to soften but their color is still bright, about 2 minutes.

2. Add the lemon juice, vinegar, brown sugar, water, and salt. Reduce the heat to medium or medium-low and gently simmer, uncovered, for about 10–15 minutes. Add the fish sauce and, using an immersion blender or a stand blender, purée the sauce until smooth. (If you are not using the sauce right away, store it in the refrigerator for up to 2 weeks in an airtight jar or plastic container. This is great on wings, but also wonderful on grilled chicken, fish, or vegetables.)

3. For the wings: Preheat the oven to 425°. Generously spray two 13 × 18-inch sheet pans with nonstick cooking spray; set aside. If the wings are whole, you may want to separate them into drumettes (the tiny drumsticks) and wing flats (the other, flat half of the wing). To do this, use kitchen scissors to snip off the wing tips, then a large chef's knife to separate the drumettes from the flats. (If this seems like too much bother, you can leave the wings whole.)

4. Place the wings in a large bowl and dry them very well with paper towels. Sprinkle them with the baking powder and salt and toss to coat evenly. Place the wings on the prepared pans. Bake for 20–25 minutes, flip the wings over, and bake for 20–25 minutes longer, or until the wings are golden and the skin is crispy. Toss immediately in Piri Piri sauce and serve.

Classic Chicken and Dumplings

CONTEMPORARY **VEGETARIAN MUSHROOM STEW WITH SWEET POTATO DUMPLINGS**

INTERNATIONAL **HUNGARIAN CHICKEN PAPRIKASH WITH DUMPLINGS**

I placed a savory, steaming bowl of golden chicken and dumplings down in front of my daughter's boyfriend. It was the first time this very southern young man had come over for dinner. I made what I thought was the definitive version of chicken and dumplings; the kind I grew up eating in Columbus, Ohio. "This is delicious, Mrs. Brulé. What did you say it was?" he asked during dinner. "Chicken and dumplings," I replied, sort of baffled. "Oh. It's not like the chicken and dumplings my mom makes," he explained. "But it's good."

Of course, that set me on the hunt to understand what southern chicken and dumplings was all about. Southern chicken and dumplings is different from northern chicken and dumplings (thick, chicken stew topped with soft, puffy dumplings). Dumplings in the South are actually more like very wide, puffy noodles, cooked in the stew, rather than floating on the top. And the "stew" part does not typically use a roux or slurry (both thickening agents), so it's slightly thinner, more like soup.

Southern chicken and dumplings is old-school, double-strength chicken broth with tender, poached chicken and an ample amount of thick, soft homemade noodles or dumplings. This homespun dish needs only three or four ingredients, and your time. It's worth every minute.

The same technique is used to make sweet potato dumplings in my hearty mushroom stew. And the Chicken Paprikash (a personal favorite of mine) uses the same techniques as well. If you can make Classic Chicken and Dumplings, you will definitely be able to make all three!

opposite: Classic Chicken and Dumplings

Classic Chicken and Dumplings

🍴

Makes 8 servings

Southern dumplings are like soft little pillows blanketed in rich, velvety chicken soup. If comfort had a flavor, it would be these dumplings. Using cooled chicken stock to make the dumplings results in double-delicious chicken taste. Leaving the skin on the onion may seem odd, but it adds a pretty golden color to the stew.

1 (3–4 pound) chicken
2 celery stalks, trimmed and cut into quarters
1 medium yellow onion, peel left on, cut into quarters
8 cups chicken broth (homemade or store-bought)
2 cups all-purpose flour
1½ teaspoons kosher or sea salt

If you've bought poultry from a grocery store or farmers' market, it will have been processed properly. Rinsing chicken is not only unnecessary—it can also splash harmful bacteria around the sink, backsplash, and counters, so most experts don't recommend it these days.

Meat of any sort should only be gently simmered. Boiling can make it tough.

1 Remove the chicken from the packaging. If a bag of giblets and neck is inside the bird, take it out and discard it or freeze for making gravy. Don't rinse the chicken; just snip the trussing string from around the legs and the wings and place the chicken in a deep 8-quart pot (a stockpot or pasta pot works great for this).

2 Add the vegetables and pour in the chicken broth, making sure that it completely covers the chicken and vegetables; if necessary, add enough water to cover them.

3 Cover the pot and set it over medium-high heat. Bring just to a boil—you will know it's boiling when steam comes out from beneath the lid—then immediately turn the heat down to medium or medium-low and crack the lid of the pot. You want to keep the broth gently simmering, with constant bubbles but no vigorous bubbling. Keep the broth gently simmering this way for 1 hour.

4 Remove the chicken from the pot and set in a bowl to cool. Scoop out 1 cup of the broth and set it in the refrigerator to cool completely. Fish out the onions (don't forget their skins) and the celery with a slotted spoon and discard them. Leave the stock in the pot at room temperature for up to 1 hour while you make the dumplings.

5 Once the broth in the refrigerator is cool, make the dumplings: Combine the flour and the salt in a large bowl, then gradually add the broth, mixing with your hands. You may only need ¾ cup of the broth, so don't add it all in one go. Add just enough broth to form a stiff dough.

6 Knead the dough in the bowl until relatively smooth (it will be somewhat dimply, not perfectly smooth); cover the bowl with a kitchen towel and set aside.

7 Pull the chicken off the bones, discarding the bones and skin, and chop it or shred it by hand. Keep the meat in a large bowl in the refrigerator until ready to use.

8 Lightly flour a clean, dry surface (a countertop or kitchen table works great). Place the dough on the floured surface and lightly flour the top of the dough. Flatten the dough into a disk shape, then roll the disk with a rolling pin, pressing down as you roll, until it's about ⅛–¼ inch thick (the thickness of pie dough). Using either a pizza cutter or a table knife, cut the dough into 1-inch-wide strips, then cut each strip into 2-inch-long pieces.

9 You should have 8 cups of liquid in the pot; if you don't, add enough water to make 8 cups. Bring the broth to a strong simmer over medium-high heat. Add the dumplings, one at a time. Do not stir. Be sure to adjust the heat to keep the liquid at a constant simmer (but don't let it boil), and cook, uncovered, for 15 minutes, or until the dumplings have expanded in size and are soft. Add the shredded chicken and serve at once.

Vegetarian Mushroom Stew with Sweet Potato Dumplings

🍴

Makes 8 servings

This rich, satisfying stew isn't just for vegetarians. It's clean eating at its most delicious.

Dried porcini mushrooms have a wonderful ability to amp up the flavors of the ingredients with which they are paired. They naturally accentuate the meaty flavor of the other mushrooms in this stew.

Never wash mushrooms with water; they are such absorbent sponges that they will become soggy. It's better to gently rub them with a dry kitchen towel or paper towel to remove surface soil.

Leeks, on the other hand, are grown in sandy soil and need to be cut open and vigorously cleaned with water.

FOR THE STEW

½ ounce dried porcini mushrooms

1½ cups boiling water

2 tablespoons olive oil

2 medium leeks, white and tender green part only, chopped fine

4 fat garlic cloves, minced or pressed

2 medium/large portobello mushrooms, stems discarded,
    caps cut into ½-inch cubes
2 pounds white button mushrooms, stems discarded,
    caps chopped small
1 teaspoon kosher or sea salt
2 tablespoons dry sherry
½ cup dry white wine
12 cups mushroom or chicken broth, divided
¾ cup all-purpose flour

FOR THE DUMPLINGS
2 cups mashed and cooled sweet potatoes
½ cup freshly grated Parmesan cheese
1¼ teaspoons chopped fresh rosemary
½ teaspoon kosher or sea salt
1½ cups all-purpose flour, plus extra for rolling

HOW TO MICROWAVE A SWEET POTATO
Pierce the skin of the sweet potato all over, about 6 times, with a sharp knife or
a fork. Place on a microwavable plate and microwave at full power for 5–8 minutes
(depending on the size of the sweet potato—the larger it is, the longer it will take).
The potato is cooked when the skin is crisp and the flesh inside is completely
tender.

1 For the stew: Place the porcini mushrooms in a heat-proof bowl
   and pour the boiling water over them. This will rehydrate them
   and give you a yummy mushroom broth. Cover the bowl with a lid
   or plate and set aside for 30 minutes.
2 Pour the olive oil into a deep 8-quart pot (a stockpot or pasta pot
   works great) and set it over medium heat. When the oil starts to
   dimple, add the leeks and the garlic and sauté for 2 minutes, or
   until soft but not colored.

3 Add the portobello and button mushrooms, raise the heat to medium-high, sprinkle with salt, and stir occasionally. The mushrooms will begin to look wet and become soft as they release their liquid. Reduce the heat to medium and cook, with lid cracked, for 5–10 minutes, or until the mushrooms release their liquid, stirring occasionally.

4 While the leeks and mushrooms are cooking, pull the porcini mushrooms out of the soaking water. Don't simply dump them into a sieve—there will be grit and sand in the bottom of the bowl. You can get rid of this grit by using a homemade filter: Fold two paper towels into an approximately 3 × 3-inch square and wet it, then wring it dry. Place the damp paper towels over a clean coffee mug or bowl, letting the towel droop a bit in the middle. Pour the porcini soaking liquid through the wet paper towels into the cup or bowl; the towels will catch the grit. Set the grit-free soaking liquid aside. Mince the porcinis.

5 Add the porcinis, soaking liquid, salt, sherry, and white wine to the simmering mushrooms. Simmer for 10 minutes.

6 In a small bowl, combine 1 cup of the mushroom or chicken broth with the flour and stir until smooth. This mixture, called a slurry, will be a thickening agent.

7 Add the remaining mushroom or chicken broth to the simmering mushrooms, then add the slurry. Stir, bring to a gentle simmer, and cook for 10 minutes. Reduce the heat to medium.

8 While the stew is simmering, make the dumplings: Stir all the ingredients together in a large bowl until smooth.

9 Heavily flour a clean, dry surface (a countertop or kitchen table works great). Place the sticky dough ball on the floured surface and heavily flour the top of the dough. Flatten the dough into a disk shape, then roll the disk with a rolling pin, pressing down as you roll, until the dough is about ⅛–¼ inch thick (the thickness of pie dough). Using either a pizza cutter or a table knife, cut the dough into 1-inch-wide strips, then cut each strip into 2-inch-long pieces. The dough will be sticky beneath the flour. Use a spatula to transfer the dumplings to the bubbling mushroom stew. Simmer about 5 minutes, stirring twice, until the dumplings float. Serve at once.

Hungarian Chicken Paprikash with Dumplings

This thick, brick-red stew with all its gorgeous chicken fragrance and flavor is something I dream about. I can't go more than a couple of weeks without making it.

Makes 8 servings

Paprika was one of those spices that I didn't really know what to do with until I was well into my thirties. Before that time, I regarded paprika (also known as paprikash) as nothing more than an adornment to deviled eggs or maybe cream of potato soup—a contrasting color, not a flavor.

My ideas about paprikash changed when we lived in Europe. In the Czech Republic, I tasted authentic Goulash for the first time and marveled at the rich, red stew with its comforting but not altogether familiar flavors. In Hungary, I became addicted to Chicken Paprikash; it's the perfect balance of umami and pleasing sour notes (from the sour cream).

Paprika imparts a fabulous, distinct flavor to both of these dishes. In the United States, paprika comes in three distinct types: sweet, hot, and smoked. I keep a small tin of each in my spice cupboard and use them regularly. Make sure to use a fresh tin of paprika. Hungarian paprika is considered the most pungent.

1 (3–4 pound) chicken
8 cups chicken broth (homemade or store-bought)
2 celery stalks, trimmed and cut into quarters
1 medium onion, peeled and cut into quarters
2 cups crushed (unseasoned) tomatoes
2 tablespoons sweet paprika
1 tablespoon smoked paprika
1 teaspoon kosher or sea salt
½ cup all-purpose flour
¾ cup sour cream
2 cups all-purpose flour
1½ teaspoons kosher or sea salt

1 Remove the chicken from its packaging. If a bag of giblets and neck is inside the bird, take it out and discard it or freeze it for making gravy. Don't rinse the bird; just snip off the trussing string from around the legs and the wings and place the chicken in a deep 8-quart pot (a stockpot or pasta pot works great).

2 Add the celery and onions to the pot and pour in the chicken broth, making sure that the chicken and vegetables are covered; if necessary, add enough water to cover them.

3 Cover the pot and set over medium-high heat. Bring the liquid just to a boil, then immediately turn the heat down to medium or medium-low and crack the lid of the pot. You want to keep the broth gently simmering, with constant bubbles but no vigorous bubbling. Simmer for 1 hour.

4 Remove the chicken from the pot and set it in a bowl to cool. Scoop out 1 cup of the broth and set it in the refrigerator to cool completely. Fish out the onions and celery with a slotted spoon and discard. Leave the broth in the pot at room temperature for up to 1 hour while you make the dumplings.

5 Once the broth in the refrigerator is cool, combine the flour and salt in a large bowl, then gradually add the broth, mixing with your hands. You may only need ¾ cup of the broth, so don't add it all in one go. Add just enough broth to form a stiff dough.

6 Knead the dough in the bowl until relatively smooth (it will be somewhat dimply, not perfectly smooth). Cover the bowl with a kitchen towel and set aside.

7 Pull the chicken off the bones, discarding the bones and skin, and chop it or shred it by hand. Keep the meat in a large bowl in the refrigerator until ready to use.

8 Lightly flour a clean, dry surface (a countertop or kitchen table works great). Place the dough on the floured surface and lightly flour the top of the dough. Flatten the dough into a disk shape, then roll the disk with a rolling pin, pressing down as you roll, until the dough is about ¼–⅛ inch thick (the thickness of pie dough). Using either a pizza cutter or a table knife, cut the dough into 1-inch-wide strips, then cut each strip into 2-inch-long pieces.

9 Bring the broth to a strong simmer over medium-high heat. Meanwhile, in a large bowl, combine the crushed tomatoes, paprika, salt, and flour and stir until there are no lumps of flour. Pour this mixture into the simmering broth, reduce the heat to medium-low, and stir every few minutes. The stew should bubble but not boil. Cook for 10–20 minutes.

10 Add the dumplings, one at a time, to the simmering stew. Do not stir. Adjust the heat to keep the stew at a constant simmer (but don't let it boil), and cook, uncovered, for 15 minutes, or until the dumplings have expanded in size and are soft. Remove the stew from the heat and stir in the sour cream, followed by the shredded chicken. Serve at once.

Classic Smothered Pork Chops

CONTEMPORARY

ROAST PORK TENDERLOIN WITH CHIMICHURRI

INTERNATIONAL

ITALIAN PORK CHOPS WITH SAFFRON TOMATO SAUCE AND PROVOLONE

The rich, umami-filled scent of roasting pork is one of my all-time favorite kitchen smells. Pork chops are a classic for good reason. They are an economical, flavorful source of protein.

Choosing "bone-in" chops will add flavor to the dish, but some find boneless chops easier to handle.

The tenderloin is the "filet mignon" of the pork—lean, tender, and quicker to cook than chops. It doesn't quite have the flavor that chops do, but it's very easy to prepare—a great choice if you want to get dinner on the table in under 30 minutes. A whole tenderloin can also be cut into 2-inch medallions, then seared on the stove top with olive oil and garlic. In mere minutes, you'll have a nutritious, restaurant-quality meal.

The recipe for chops with saffron, tomato sauce, and provolone features some of my favorite Italian flavors, from both the north and the south of that gorgeous country.

opposite: Classic Smothered Pork Chops

Classic Smothered Pork Chops

🍴

Makes 4 servings

My friend Laura Ashley is a petite, fair-haired firecracker of a woman. She's an awe-inspiring conversationalist who has never met a stranger. Growing up in Raleigh, North Carolina, she ate all of the classic recipes I present in this book, so I couldn't think of anyone better than Laura Ashley and her family to test some of them. What I did not know was that she didn't know how to cook. I mean this literally (and she freely admits it).

The evening she made these smothered pork chops for her husband and two children, she texted me (in all caps), "THIS IS THE FIRST TIME I'VE EVER COOKED MEAT, OTHER THAN A TURKEY AT THANKSGIVING! THIS IS GOING TO BE A DISASTER!" I texted back that she only needed to follow the directions and trust herself, and everything would turn out just fine.

An hour later, I received another text: "That was the best thing I've ever tasted! We ate all the chops, then I drank the gravy! I'm so proud!"

    1 teaspoon kosher or sea salt
    1 teaspoon garlic powder
    1 teaspoon onion powder
    ½ teaspoon smoked paprika
    ½ teaspoon freshly cracked black pepper
    4 pork chops, 1–2 inches thick, bone-in (if possible)
    ½ cup all-purpose flour
    ⅓ cup vegetable oil
    1 small yellow onion, peeled, cut in half (root to tip)
        and sliced into thin half-moons (about 2 cups)
    1 small green bell pepper, seeds and stem removed,
        sliced into thin strips
    1½ cups chicken broth
    ½ cup buttermilk (not fat-free)

1 Mix the salt, garlic powder, onion powder, paprika, and pepper together in a small bowl. Sprinkle evenly over both sides of the chops, using all of the seasoning.

2 Pour the flour onto a dinner plate or pie plate. Dredge the seasoned chops in the flour, one at a time, patting the flour all over them, lightly shaking any excess flour back onto the plate. Place the dredged chops on a separate plate as you go. Reserve 2 tablespoons of the flour and discard the rest.

3 Pour 2 tablespoons of the oil into a 10-inch cast-iron skillet or heavy sauté pan and place it over medium heat. When the oil starts to dimple, add the chops and allow them to cook, uncovered, undisturbed for 5 minutes. You may only have room to cook two chops at a time. Flip the chops; if the pan is dry, add 1 more tablespoon of oil. Cook for 5 minutes. At this point the chops will be browned, but not cooked through. Repeat with any remaining chops.

4 Remove the chops from the skillet and place them on a dinner plate. If the pan is dry, add 1 tablespoon of the oil. Add the onions and green peppers, raise the heat to medium-high, and sauté, stirring often, until they are soft, about 10 minutes. Add the reserved dredging flour to the onions/peppers and sauté for 1 more minute. Add the chicken broth, reduce the heat to medium, and cook for about 2 minutes, stirring constantly, until the sauce thickens and coats the back of a spoon, like a cream soup. Return the chops and any juices that have accumulated around them to the pan, coat with the sauce, cover, and reduce the heat to medium-low or low. It's fine if the chops overlap; just rearrange them halfway through the cooking time. Simmer them very gently for 45 minutes. The chops will become firm and turn from pink to white.

5 Remove the chops from the skillet and add the buttermilk. Bring the sauce just to a simmer and taste it—you may want to add ¼ –½ teaspoon salt. Return the chops to the pan and turn them to coat in the sauce. Serve at once.

Roast Pork Tenderloin with Chimichurri

Makes 4–6 servings

My daughter Camille's first school experience was in Switzerland. She attended a sweet preschool in a little cottage that was so quaint it felt like stepping into a fairy-tale book every time I took her there. I also became good friends with many of the other mommies whose children were in preschool. Most of us are still friends today.

Martina, the mother of Camille's friend Leila, was from Argentina and owned a public relations company in Zürich. She was tall, blonde, and drop-dead gorgeous—and multilingual too. Those two years I spent in remedial high school French made this a quality I greatly admired. I once asked Martina how many languages she knew. This was her completely serious answer: "You see, I can speak five—Spanish, Italian, German, English, and French—but I can only negotiate in three."

Martina would tell stories about the wonderful dishes she grew up eating in her home country, and it seemed chimichurri was often in the mix.

Chimichurri is a classic Argentinean green sauce made from fresh herbs (most commonly oregano) and sherry vinegar. In Argentina it's typically served with beef, but I think its pungent, tart, fabulous flavor makes it perfect on virtually any grilled or roasted meat, poultry, or fish. It also makes a superb salad dressing.

Pork tenderloin is one of the easiest cuts of meat to cook because it comes trimmed and lean from the meat department. It should be served still pink and juicy in the middle. Although it works great on the grill, this recipe calls for oven-roasting (which is even easier). Tenderloins usually come in packs of two, which is an ample amount for six people.

FOR THE CHIMICHURRI
3 tablespoons sherry vinegar
½ teaspoon kosher or sea salt
3 tablespoons roughly chopped shallots
3 fat garlic cloves, roughly chopped
¼ cup flat-leaf parsley
2 tablespoons fresh oregano leaves
2 teaspoons red pepper flakes
½ cup extra-virgin olive oil

FOR THE TENDERLOINS
1 teaspoon kosher or sea salt
1 teaspoon garlic powder
1 teaspoon onion powder
½ teaspoon freshly cracked black pepper
2 pork tenderloins (one package)
¼ cup extra-virgin olive oil, or more as needed

1 For the chimichurri: Whisk the vinegar and salt together in a small bowl until the salt dissolves.
2 Place the salted vinegar, shallot, garlic, parsley, oregano, and red pepper flakes into the bowl of a food processor and pulse 4 times, just to finely chop.
3 Add the oil and process for just a few seconds. Pour the chimichurri into a bowl and leave at room temperature until ready to use (up to 2 hours). Otherwise, refrigerate for up to 3 days, but bring to room temperature before serving. Makes about ¾ cup, which should be enough for about 12 servings.
4 For the tenderloin: Preheat the oven to 425°. Mix the salt, garlic powder, onion powder, and pepper together in a small bowl. Pat the seasoning evenly onto both tenderloins; be sure to use all of it.

5 Spray a jelly roll pan with nonstick cooking spray; set aside. Pour the oil into a 10-inch cast-iron skillet or heavy sauté pan and place it over medium heat. When the oil starts to dimple, add one of the tenderloins and brown it on all three sides (about 2 minutes per side) and transfer it to the prepared pan. If the skillet or sauté pan gets dry, add 1 more tablespoon of oil before cooking the second tenderloin. The tenderloins will be browned but not cooked through. Place the tenderloins on the prepared pan and roast until the internal
temperature of each reads 145°, about 15–20 minutes.

6 Remove the tenderloins from the oven and allow them to "rest" (a chef-y word for "cool") for 5–10 minutes, then slice and drizzle with the chimichurri.

Italian Pork Chops with
Saffron Tomato Sauce and Provolone

If you can make southern smothered chops, you can make this, too. It's a mash-up between southern Italian and northern Italian cuisines, using tomatoes (southern), pork, saffron, and provolone cheese (northern). The result is sublime—perfect for a dinner party.

Makes 4 servings

  1½ teaspoons kosher or sea salt, divided
  ½ teaspoon freshly cracked black pepper
  4 pork chops, 1–2 inch thick, bone-in (if possible)
  ½ cup all-purpose flour
  ⅓ cup olive oil
  ½ cup finely minced shallots
  3–4 fat garlic cloves, minced or pressed (about 2 tablespoons)
  ½ cup dry white wine
  ⅛ teaspoon saffron powder or ¼ teaspoon saffron threads
  1 (15-ounce) can diced tomatoes with juice
  4 slices provolone cheese

1. Season both sides of the chops with 1 teaspoon of the salt and the pepper.

2. Pour the flour onto a dinner plate or pie plate. Dredge the seasoned chops, one at a time, in the flour, patting the flour all over the chops, lightly shaking off excess flour back onto the plate. Place the dredged chops on a separate plate as you go.

3. Pour 2 tablespoons of the olive oil into a 10-inch cast-iron skillet or heavy sauté pan and place over medium heat. When the oil starts to dimple, add the dredged chops and allow to cook uncovered and undisturbed for 5 minutes. You may only have room to cook two chops at a time. Flip the chops; if the pan is dry, add 1 more tablespoon of the oil. Cook for 5 minutes. At this point the chops will be lightly browned, but not cooked through. Repeat with any remaining chops.

4. Remove the chops from the skillet and place them on a dinner plate. If the pan is dry, add 1 tablespoon of the oil. Add the shallots and garlic and raise the heat to medium-high. Sauté until the shallots become translucent and the garlic is fragrant. Add the white wine and stir, scraping up the brown bits at the bottom of the pan with a wooden spoon or rubber spatula; this is called deglazing the pan. Add the saffron, the remaining salt, and the tomatoes with their juice, turning up the heat to medium-high and allowing the sauce to strongly simmer (not quite boiling), uncovered, for 5 minutes.

5 Return the chops to the pan and coat with the sauce. Cover the pan and reduce the heat to medium-low or low. It's fine if the chops overlap—just rearrange them halfway through the cooking time. Simmer, very gently, for 45 minutes.

6 Remove the chops from the skillet, place them on a dinner plate, and cover with foil to keep warm. Increase the heat to high and boil the sauce for 7 minutes, or until it's reduced and thickened to the consistency of a cream soup. Return the chops to the pan and lay one slice of the provolone cheese on each chop, reduce the heat to medium-low, cover the pan, and cook gently just until the cheese melts, about 5 minutes. Serve each chop on top of the tomato sauce.

Classic Chicken-Fried Steak with Gravy

CONTEMPORARY OVEN-FRIED STEAK WITH GRAVY

INTERNATIONAL MOJO MARINATED CUBAN STEAK

If crispy fried chicken and juicy steak had a baby, it would be chicken-fried steak—crunchy on the outside, tender and beefy within, and then coated with creamy pan gravy. If you want to impress a friend or sweetheart, this is the dish to make.

Chicken-fried steak and country-fried steak are almost interchangeable names. Country-fried is the original name for cube steak that's been breaded and fried, but in the twentieth century, in some parts of the South, the "chicken-fried" title was introduced (probably because of the similar preparation to frying chicken). Country-fried steaks are often finished by simmering in the pan gravy, but I prefer to drizzle the gravy on top just before serving, to preserve the steak's crunch.

Cube steak is the cut of beef cooks most often use when making chicken-fried steak. It's a top sirloin or top round steak (both tough cuts of beef) that has been tenderized through pounding with a meat mallet or an electric tenderizer. The small indentations made in the process are in the shape of cubes, hence the name.

The contemporary version is just as tasty; the fat in the classic version has been replaced by the umami-packed flavor of fish sauce, which is important in this recipe. The Mojo Marinated Cuban Steak is redolent of garlic and Caribbean-inspired flavors.

opposite: Classic Chicken-Fried Steak with Gravy

Classic Chicken-Fried Steak with Gravy

Makes 4 servings

A crisp crust giving way to savory, tender beef—that is what chicken-fried steak is all about. It's divine. Using cornstarch in the initial breading ensures crispiness.

1 cup all-purpose flour
1 cup cornstarch
1 teaspoon onion powder
1 teaspoon garlic powder
2 eggs
½ cup buttermilk or milk
1 cup peanut or vegetable oil for frying, plus more if needed
4 cube steaks
1½ cups chicken broth
2 tablespoons heavy cream
¼ teaspoon kosher or sea salt
⅛ teaspoon freshly cracked black pepper

If you don't have a candy thermometer, you can determine whether the oil is hot enough for frying the old-school way: Heat the oil, covered, over medium heat for about 5–7 minutes, then flick a few drops of water into it. If the water makes the oil bubble steadily, it's ready for frying; if the oil crackles wildly, it's too hot and the heat needs to be lowered; and if the oil doesn't bubble at all, it's not hot enough yet.

1 Set up the breading station: In a pie plate, stir together the flour, cornstarch, onion powder, and garlic powder. In a second pie plate, whisk together the eggs and buttermilk.

2 Pour the oil into a 10-inch cast-iron or very heavy skillet, to come ½ inch up the side, and set it over medium heat, covered, for 5–7 minutes.

3 Preheat the oven to 250°. Fit a jelly roll pan with a wire rack. Working with one steak at a time, dredge it in the seasoned flour, pressing the flour into the meat's crevices and lightly shaking off

the excess flour. Dip the steak in the egg/buttermilk mixture, making sure to coat both sides. Finally, dredge the steak in the flour again, coating it completely. Place the steak on the wire rack and repeat with the remaining steaks. Reserve the remaining seasoned flour.

4   Once the steaks are breaded and the oil has reached 350° (use a candy thermometer, but if you don't have one, see the instructions opposite on how to know if the oil is hot enough for frying), use tongs to carefully lay the steaks in the oil. Make sure not to crowd the skillet; there will probably only be room for two medium steaks or one large one at a time. The steak should not be submerged in the oil, and the oil should be bubbling all around it. If the oil is bubbling too much, turn the heat down to medium-low—you may need to adjust the heat throughout the cooking process. Pink juices will be released through the breading as the steaks fry. This shows you that the meat is cooking. Cook for 4 minutes, then, using tongs, turn the steaks over. Take care! The oil will sputter from the steak's juices, but the sputtering will die down a few seconds after you turn each steak. Cook an additional 4 minutes. The steaks will be golden to light brown. Remove the steaks from the skillet, allowing the excess oil to drip back into the pan, and place them on a clean jelly roll pan. Put the tray of steaks in the oven and continue with the rest of the frying.

5   Remove all but 3 tablespoons of the oil from the skillet (leave all the brown bits—called the fond—in the skillet). Set the heat on medium. Add 3 tablespoons of the seasoned dredging flour to the pan and stir well, scraping up all the fond. This mixture, called a roux (equal parts fat and flour, by weight), is what will thicken the gravy. Turn the heat down to medium-low and cook the roux for 1 minute, then add the chicken broth. Stir constantly as the gravy begins to thicken. Allow the gravy to bubble gently for 2 minutes. After 2 minutes, add the cream, salt, and pepper. Stir until the sauce is relatively smooth (a few lumps are okay), with the consistency of a thick cream soup. Serve the sauce drizzled over the steaks.

Oven-Fried Steak with Gravy

🍴

Makes 4 servings

The crunch as well as the wonderfully savory beef remain in this updated version of the classic. The smoked paprika adds a wonderful umami and helps turn the steaks a more golden color. By using coconut oil rather than vegetable oil and baking rather than frying, I've taken this classic in a healthier and deliciously different direction.

1 teaspoon onion powder
1 teaspoon garlic powder
½ teaspoon kosher or sea salt
½ teaspoon freshly cracked black pepper
4 cube steaks
½ cup all-purpose flour
½ cup cornstarch
3 egg whites
1 cup buttermilk
1½ cups panko bread crumbs
½ cup fine cornmeal
½ teaspoon smoked paprika

¼ cup melted coconut oil

1 cup chicken broth

½ teaspoon fish sauce

¼ teaspoon freshly cracked black pepper

1 tablespoon heavy cream

1 Preheat the oven to 375°. Spray a jelly roll pan with nonstick cooking spray; set aside. Mix the onion powder, garlic powder, salt, and pepper together in a small bowl. Sprinkle each side of the steaks with about ¼ teaspoon of this seasoning and set aside. (You will have some of the seasoning left over.)

2 Set up the breading station: In a pie plate, stir together the flour and cornstarch. In a second pie plate, whisk together the egg whites and buttermilk. In a third pie plate, toss together the bread crumbs, cornmeal, and paprika.

3 Bread the steaks: Place the seasoned steaks, one at a time, in the flour/cornstarch mixture. Pack the mixture into the meat's crevices and shake off the excess, then dip the steaks in the egg/buttermilk mixture, making sure to coat each steak completely. Finally, coat the steaks evenly with the bread crumb mixture. Place the steaks on the prepared pan and drizzle each side of the steaks with 1½ teaspoons of the coconut oil. Rub the oil into the coating with the back of a spoon to spread evenly. Bake the steaks for 15 minutes, flip them over, and bake them 10–15 minutes longer, or until they are golden.

4 While the steaks are baking, make the gravy: In a jar with a tight-fitting lid, shake together the chicken broth, 1 tablespoon of the remaining flour/cornstarch mixture, and the fish sauce. Pour the mixture into a small sauce pot and set it over medium heat, stirring frequently. When the gravy comes to a simmer, allow it to bubble gently for about 2 minutes, stirring often. Remove the pot from the heat, stir in the pepper and heavy cream, and serve the gravy over the steaks.

Mojo Marinated Cuban Steak

Makes 4 servings

Mojo (a Spanish word pronounced *Mo*-ho) is a Cuban sauce made of garlic, citrus juice, and olive oil. My interpretation adds the earthy flavor of cumin. This sauce tastes truly tropical and also makes a great marinade for other grilled meats, poultry, or seafood.

The marinating time in this recipe is short due to the high proportion of citrus juice. The more acid (citrus, vinegar, or wine, for example) in a marinade, the faster it will tenderize the protein (meat, poultry, or seafood). Too long in this tart marinade, however, can actually toughen the meat, so longer isn't better (especially with delicate proteins like poultry, and even more so with seafood). Here's a good general rule of thumb when it comes to marinating: The denser or larger the protein, the longer it needs to be marinated. In other words, you shouldn't marinate raw shrimp nearly as long as a flank steak.

¼ cup lime juice

Juice of two navel oranges (about ½ cup)

4 garlic cloves, minced or pressed

¼ teaspoon ground cumin

2 tablespoons chopped fresh cilantro, plus more for garnish

¾ cup extra-virgin olive oil

4 cube steaks

2 tablespoons vegetable or peanut oil

1 Whisk together the lime and orange juices, garlic, cumin, and cilantro, then slowly whisk in the olive oil. Pour the marinade into a casserole dish and add the cube steaks, submerging them as well as possible. Cover the dish with plastic wrap and marinate at room temperature for 30 minutes.

2 Remove the steaks from the marinade and dry very well with paper towels. Pour the vegetable or peanut oil into a 10-inch cast-iron or very heavy skillet and place it over medium heat. When the oil starts to dimple, add the steaks and cook, uncovered, for just 2 minutes per side. The steaks will release liquid and braise in their own juices. Serve at once with a scattering of chopped cilantro.

Classic Golden Fried Fish

CONTEMPORARY **QUINOA-CRUSTED BAKED FISH**

INTERNATIONAL **THAI FISH CAKES**

Southern fried fish should be very light and crisp, just like Classic Southern Fried Chicken, but with the added crunch of cornmeal. There are "fish camps" all over the South—casual places, often out in the middle of nowhere, where families go for dinner or after church on Sunday afternoon to fill up on tender, crispy fried fish. Frying fish is really quite quick and surprisingly simple to do at home. As when you fry chicken, it's important to keep your eye on the oil temperature: If it's too hot, the crust will burn before the fish is cooked; if it's not hot enough, the fish will poach in the oil rather than fry, resulting in greasy, soggy fish.

Like all of the contemporary-styled recipes in this book, the quinoa-crusted fish is just as delicious as the fried. The Thai fish cakes are surprisingly quick and easy to pull together and make beautiful little hors d'oeuvres.

opposite: Classic Golden Fried Fish

Classic Golden Fried Fish

Makes 2–4 servings

If you've never tried southern fried fish, you are in for a treat. It's noticeably lighter than, say, British fish and chips, because southern fried fish doesn't use a batter, which creates a thick crust; instead it calls for just a dusting of flour and cornmeal. With a squeeze of fresh lemon juice, it's a wonderful way to enjoy fish.

1 teaspoon garlic powder
1 teaspoon onion powder
½ teaspoon kosher or sea salt
½ teaspoon freshly cracked black pepper
1–2 cups peanut oil
1 pound white fish fillets (flounder, grouper, or catfish)
½ cup fine cornmeal (yellow or white)
¼ cup all-purpose flour
½ teaspoon paprika
Popcorn salt
1 lemon, cut into wedges

1 Preheat the oven to 250°. Fit a jelly roll pan with a wire rack. Mix the garlic powder, onion powder, salt, and pepper together in a small bowl. Set aside.

2 Set a 10-inch cast-iron or very heavy skillet over medium heat. Pour in enough oil to come ½ inch up the side, then cover the skillet. Allow the oil to heat for 5–7 minutes. Season both sides of the fish fillets with the garlic powder mixture.

3 Stir together the cornmeal, flour, and paprika in a large bowl or dinner plate.

4 Uncover the skillet and flick water from your fingers into the oil. If it bubbles quickly, it's ready. Dredge both sides of the fillets in the cornmeal mixture and use tongs to lay them in the oil. Don't crowd the skillet—there should be at least 1 inch of space between the fillets, so there may only be room for two at a time. The oil should be bubbling rapidly all around each fillet. Fry for 4 minutes on the first side, gently turn the fillets over with tongs, and fry the other side for 4 minutes. Remove the fish from the skillet and place it on the wire rack. Season the fillets lightly with popcorn salt and keep them in the warm oven as you fry the rest of the fish. Serve with lemon wedges.

Quinoa-Crusted Baked Fish

Makes 2–4 servings

The three-step breading method is what creates a wonderful crust on this healthy baked fish. In this method, the first dredge in cornstarch gives the egg wash something to cling to, so that the final crunchy quinoa-flake coating will stick securely to the egg. It's like all the coatings are hugging each other. Don't skip the cornstarch dredge: If you do, the egg wash will slip right off the fish.

Quinoa flakes are different from ordinary quinoa (that round seed that looks like couscous). The flakes are made from the seed but are lighter and perfect to use as a coating when a crunchy exterior is desired. You can find quinoa flakes in the baking section of many supermarkets and most natural food stores.

1 teaspoon garlic powder
1 teaspoon onion powder
½ teaspoon kosher or sea salt
½ teaspoon freshly cracked black pepper
¾ cup cornstarch
1 cup fine cornmeal (yellow or white)
½ cup quinoa flakes
1 teaspoon paprika

1 egg, whisked

½ cup buttermilk

1 pound white fish fillets (flounder, grouper, or catfish)

¼ cup melted coconut oil (you may have some left over)

1 Preheat the oven to 425°. Spray a jelly roll pan with nonstick cooking spray. Mix the garlic powder, onion powder, salt, and pepper together in a small bowl. Set aside.

2 Set up the breading station: Place the cornstarch in a pie plate or dinner plate. In a second pie plate, mix together the cornmeal, quinoa flakes, and paprika. In a third pie plate, whisk together the eggs and buttermilk.

3 Dry the fish fillets between paper towels and season both sides with the garlic powder mixture. Dredge the fish, one fillet at a time, in the cornstarch, shaking off the excess. Dip the fillet in the egg mixture (making sure it's well coated) and then coat it in the cornmeal mixture. Lay the fillets on the prepared pan as you go.

4 Drizzle ½–1 teaspoon of the coconut oil on the top of each fillet and rub the oil evenly into the breading with the back of a spoon. Bake for 25 minutes. The fish will be tender on the inside, with a crunchy exterior, though not as pretty and golden as the fried version. Serve at once.

Quinoa-Crusted Baked Fish

Thai Fish Cakes

*Makes about
2 dozen small cakes*

Savory, slightly sweet, and tangy, these pale green Thai fish cakes flecked with bits of red bell pepper are as pretty as they are delicious. The white fish and shrimp give these little fish cakes a nice texture. They are great served for dinner with rice, or passed around as an appetizer.

1 pound white fish fillets (flounder, cod, grouper, or catfish)

½ pound raw shrimp, peeled and deveined

3 green onions, including green tops, trimmed and chopped

½ small red bell pepper, roughly chopped

Zest of ½ lime, chopped

1–2 teaspoons roughly chopped fresh ginger root

½ cup roughly chopped fresh cilantro

1 tablespoon fish sauce

2 teaspoons soy sauce

2 teaspoons lightly packed light brown sugar

1–2 teaspoons green curry paste

1 egg

1 Place all of the ingredients except the egg in the bowl of a food processor and process until well chopped, about 20 seconds. Scrape down the sides of the bowl, add the egg, and process again for 10 seconds, until you have a thick, chunky fish paste. Move the paste to a bowl, cover, and refrigerate for at least 30 minutes, up to 24 hours.

2 Preheat the oven to 250°. Set a cast-iron or very heavy skillet over medium heat and spray liberally with nonstick cooking spray. Wet your hands and shape the fish paste into small patties, about 2 inches in diameter and ½ inch thick. Don't crowd the pan; fry only as many as will comfortably fit in the pan at one time. Sauté the patties until golden on one side, about 3 minutes, then flip them and sauté the other side for 3 minutes. Watch the heat: You may need to lower it to just a smidge below medium if the cakes seem to be cooking too quickly. Keep the cooked cakes warm in the oven until all the sautéing is done.

Classic Fried Green Tomatoes

CONTEMPORARY **OVEN-FRIED GREEN TOMATOES**

INTERNATIONAL **GRILLED GREEN TOMATO SALSA**

Green tomatoes are simply unripe tomatoes. Because they're not yet ripe, they are fairly sour and very firm—they hold up beautifully not only to frying but also to grilling (as you'll see in the grilled salsa recipe). Fried green tomatoes are seasoned and coated in cornmeal before frying. The cornmeal ensures a toothsome crunch.

One mistake that many people make when storing tomatoes (green or ripe) is to put them in the refrigerator. Refrigerating tomatoes makes them mealy and grainy and diminishes their flavor tremendously. Always keep tomatoes of any color, size, or ripeness at room temperature on the kitchen counter or windowsill, stem-side down.

Oven-Fried Green Tomatoes make a wonderful, healthy sandwich, layered with turkey bacon on toast with lettuce. Grilling green tomatoes brings a sassiness to your salsa.

Classic Fried Green Tomatoes

Makes 6 servings

The farmer from whom I loyally buy tomatoes at our weekly farmers' market let me in on a secret that changed the way I cook fried green tomatoes: Fry them when they are just past green, turning toward yellow. Tomatoes (and most other vegetables) ripen from green to yellow to red. When most varieties of tomatoes (not actual yellow tomatoes) are just starting to turn yellow, they are still firm enough to stand up to frying, yet slightly softer and sweeter than bright green. At that point in the ripening process the tomato's texture is almost velvety. Look for green tomatoes that are just starting to turn yellow on their tips—opposite from the stem. Streaks of yellow are fine, but no more than that.

If you can only find green tomatoes, buy them and let them sit on your kitchen counter, stem-side down, for a day or two until they become greenish-yellow.

3 medium green/yellow tomatoes
Kosher or sea salt
1–2 cups vegetable or peanut oil
¼ cup all-purpose flour
¼ cup cornstarch
½ teaspoon garlic powder
¾ cup finely ground cornmeal
¾ cup panko bread crumbs
1 egg
½ cup buttermilk
Popcorn salt

1 Trim the stem end out of the tomatoes and slice them crosswise in ½-inch slices. You should get about 4–5 slices per tomato. Lightly salt the tomato slices and set them on a dinner plate lined with a double layer of paper towels for 10 minutes. The paper towels will absorb some of the tomatoes' liquid, and that will make them fry up crispier.

2 Pour the oil into a 10-inch cast-iron or very heavy skillet. The oil should come ¼ inch up the inside of the skillet because you'll be shallow frying or pan frying the tomatoes—that is, you'll fry one side at a time. Set the heat to just a smidge below medium, cover the skillet, and let the oil heat up for about 5 minutes. Meanwhile, set up your breading station: In a pie plate, mix the flour, cornstarch, and garlic powder together. In a second pie plate, mix the cornmeal and bread crumbs together. In a third pie plate, whisk the egg and buttermilk together.

3 When the oil reaches 350–375°, it will looked dimpled. At that point, flick a few drops of water into the oil. If it bubbles, it's ready. You'll be able to fry about 4 slices at a time, and you should bread only as many slices of the tomato as you can fry in one batch. Working with one slice at a time, dip the tomato slice in the flour/cornstarch mixture, coating it well on both sides (the tomato needs the flour to hold the egg/milk mixture on). Dip it in the egg/milk mixture and turn to coat both sides. Finally, dredge the tomato in the cornmeal/panko mixture, coating both sides. Continue with the other 3 slices.

4 Carefully lay the breaded tomato slices in the skillet (you can do this with tongs if you are nervous about the hot oil). The oil should bubble quickly around the tomato slices. If it doesn't, it's not hot enough. Cook for about 4 minutes. The oil should be bubbling constantly—you may need to adjust the heat, but it should remain around medium. Flip the slices and cook the other side for 4 minutes. (Don't turn the slices again—fry each side only once.) They will turn a beautiful golden color. Remove them from the pan, place them on a wire rack or a dinner plate lined with paper towels, and sprinkle with the popcorn salt. Continue this process with the rest of the tomato slices.

Oven-Fried Green Tomatoes

Makes 4–6 servings

Fat = Flavor. This is the first thing I learned in culinary school, and it truly is fundamental to cooking. So when fat is taken out of a dish, it needs to be replaced with other flavors. In this recipe, I've added two secret weapons from my culinary arsenal: smoked paprika and fish sauce. Fish sauce? Yes! It simply adds umami without any fishiness at all. The smoked paprika amps up the depth of flavor too. It's well worth having a tin in your spice cupboard. Don't be alarmed if your baked tomatoes don't turn that lovely golden brown that the classic fried tomatoes do. Because I've cut the fat, they are still crunchy and delicious, just a bit pale.

> 3 medium green/yellow tomatoes
> 1 teaspoon fish sauce
> 1 teaspoon garlic powder
> 1 teaspoon onion powder
> ⅛ teaspoon smoked paprika
> ⅛ teaspoon cayenne pepper

½ cup all-purpose flour
½ cup cornstarch
1 cup finely ground cornmeal
1 cup panko bread crumbs
2 teaspoons sweet paprika
1 egg
½ cup buttermilk
2 tablespoons melted coconut oil
Popcorn salt

1 Preheat the oven to 400°. Trim the stem end out of the tomatoes and slice them crosswise in ½-inch slices. You should get about 4–5 slices per tomato. Lay the tomato slices on a dinner plate lined with a double layer of paper towels, and drizzle the fish sauce over one side. Allow them to sit for 10 minutes. The paper towels will absorb some of the tomatoes' liquid, which will make the tomatoes bake up crispier. Stir the garlic powder, onion powder, smoked paprika, and cayenne together in a small bowl. Set aside.

2 Set up your breading station: In a pie plate, mix the flour and cornstarch together. In a second pie plate, mix the cornmeal, bread crumbs, and sweet paprika together. In a third pie plate, whisk the egg and buttermilk together. Blot the tomatoes dry with a paper towel, then sprinkle them evenly with the garlic powder mixture. Fold up a paper towel and dip the corner into the melted coconut oil so that it absorbs about a third of the oil, then use it to grease a sheet pan.

3 Dredge the tomato slices in the flour/cornstarch mixture, then in the egg/buttermilk mixture (make sure the slices are completely coated), and finally in the bread crumb/cornmeal mix. Set the breaded slices on the prepared pan. When all the tomato slices are breaded, drizzle the remaining melted coconut oil over them, followed by a good coating of nonstick cooking spray or olive oil spray. Bake for 10 minutes. Spray them with more nonstick cooking spray or olive oil spray, flip them over, and bake for 10 minutes longer. Remove them from the oven and sprinkle with popcorn salt.

Grilled Green Tomato Salsa

Makes about 3 cups

This salsa tastes spicy, tart, and fresh. It's different than classic red to-mato salsa, but equally appealing. Grilling tames the green tomatoes' tartness by concentrating the fruit's natural sugars. This is a beauti-ful salsa, not only for tortilla chips but also served with grilled fish, chicken, or meat.

1 poblano pepper
1 jalapeño pepper
4 medium green tomatoes
1 medium sweet onion (such as Vidalia)
¼ cup vegetable or olive oil
2 tablespoons lime juice
1 teaspoon kosher or sea salt
1 tablespoon agave nectar or honey
¼ teaspoon ground cumin
1 fat clove garlic
1 teaspoon fish sauce
¼ cup chopped fresh cilantro

1 Preheat the oven to 425°. Rub the poblano and jalapeño peppers lightly with oil, set them on a jelly roll pan, and bake until charred (mostly black) on all sides, about 35–45 minutes. You won't need to flip or turn them. Remove the peppers from the oven and place them in a bowl; cover with a lid or plastic wrap and let sit for 20 minutes; this will steam the skin, making it easy to peel off. If you would rather roast the peppers outside, you can place the dry (not oiled) peppers directly on the grill and cook them, turning them with tongs, until they are charred on all sides. Place the peppers in a covered bowl, as above, to steam off the skin.

2 Slice the tomatoes and onion ¾ inch thick. Set a grill pan, gas grill, or charcoal grill to high heat. Once the grill is very hot, lightly brush both sides of the tomato and the onion slices with the oil and grill until they have grill marks: 3–4 minutes per side for the tomatoes, and 5 minutes per side for the onions. Remove the slices from the grill, allow them to cool for 5 minutes, then chop them into cubes. Place them in a small bowl and set aside.

3 Rub the skin off the roasted peppers. Pull the stem ends off and slice each pepper open with a knife; scrape out and discard all of the seeds. Finely chop the peppers and toss them with the onions and tomatoes.

4 In a medium bowl, whisk together the lime juice and salt until the salt dissolves, then add the agave or honey, cumin, garlic, fish sauce, and cilantro. Add to the tomato/onion mixture and serve immediately. You can also cover the salsa and store it in the refrigerator for up to 3 days. If you refrigerate the salsa, bring it to room temperature before serving it over grilled meats, on fish tacos, or simply with tortilla chips.

Classic Green Beans

CONTEMPORARY **ROASTED GREEN BEANS WITH LEMON, GARLIC, AND PARMESAN**

INTERNATIONAL **SPICY SZECHUAN GREEN BEANS**

The snap of a fresh raw green bean signifies summer to me. Crisp and bright green, the bean has beautiful benefits that are more than skin deep. Green beans (also known as string beans) are naturally fat-free, are packed with vitamins and minerals and fiber, and are a very good source of carotenoids, an antioxidant also found in carrots and tomatoes.

In addition, green beans have a fabulous flavor and magical texture that can change depending on how they're cooked. For instance, roasting green beans dries them a bit, yielding a wonderful, slightly chewy texture, while simmering them results in an ever-so-soft bean flavored by their simmering liquid. High-temperature wok cooking will char them, adding an almost smoky flavor to the Szechuan version.

Fresh green beans are available year-round in most of the country, but if you can't find them fresh in your market, that's okay: Frozen green beans retain almost all of the same nutritional benefits, although their texture is different. Avoid using canned green beans if possible because the nutritional benefits are all but cooked out during the canning process, and they are often high in sodium.

Classic Green Beans

Makes 6 side-dish servings

My parents went through a countercultural phase in the '70s, and with that came a vegetarian, often vegan, diet for our family of seven: We went from golden roast chicken and potatoes to nut loaf and undercooked green beans. Although my parents continued with Transcendental Meditation and yoga, they left behind their groovy recipes and renewed my faith in food when they took off for Paris one summer in the '80s to study cooking at Le Cordon Bleu. So long, tough, undercooked green beans!

Food memories linger, and the woody green beans of my youth kept that wonderful vegetable out of my cooking repertoire until I moved to the South. Fresh green beans simmered simply in water with smoked meat until soft and savory have been my children's favorite since their baby days. Now they are mine too.

8 cups hot water
1 smoked ham hock, 1 smoked turkey neck or wing,
    or 4 slices bacon, chopped into ½-inch pieces
2 pounds fresh green beans, stem ends trimmed off
1 teaspoon kosher or sea salt
½ teaspoon freshly cracked black pepper

1 Place a 4- to 5-quart pot over medium-high heat and pour in enough of the hot water (it may not be all 8 cups) to fill three-quarters of the pot. Add the ham hock, turkey, or bacon, cover the pan, bring to a simmer, uncover, and cook for 30 minutes. This is the cooking liquid that will season the green beans.

2 After 30 minutes, the cooking water will have become cloudy and you will be able to smell the smoky meat. Add the beans, making sure they are submerged in the liquid. Cover the pot and bring the beans to a boil, then immediately lower the heat so that the beans are just gently simmering. You can also control the heat by cracking the lid just a bit. Cook 45 minutes to 1 hour, or until the beans are very soft but aren't falling apart.

3 Remove the pot from the heat and pull out the ham hock or turkey; set aside to cool for 10 minutes. (If you're using bacon, skip this step.) Pick some of the meat from the bones using a sharp knife. (This step is optional, but tasty.) Pull the beans from the pot and put them in a serving bowl. Toss with the salt, pepper, and picked meat, if using, and ladle about 1 cup of the cooking liquid over them. Serve at once.

Roasted Green Beans with Lemon, Garlic, and Parmesan

Makes 6 servings

Roasting virtually any vegetable can take it to a new level of deliciousness. Roasting concentrates foods' flavors in a way that simmering in water simply can't do. This recipe is good enough to be a main course, but it also does beautifully in a supporting role with seafood, poultry, or meat. I love these so much I even use up the leftovers by heating them slightly, then layering them in a sandwich with smoked turkey and Dijon mustard.

2 pounds fresh green beans, stem ends trimmed off
¼ cup plus 1 tablespoon extra-virgin olive oil
1 teaspoon kosher or sea salt
3 fat garlic cloves, minced (about 1 tablespoon)
Zest of ½ large lemon
⅓ cup freshly grated Parmesan cheese

1 Preheat the oven to 425°. Lay the green beans on a jelly roll pan and drizzle with ¼ cup of the oil. Toss the beans and oil with your hands so that all of the beans are coated, then sprinkle them with the salt. Roast for 15 minutes. Roasting will fade the beans' color from a bright green to a paler green, and they will begin to shrivel up a bit.

2 While the beans are roasting, mince the garlic and lemon zest together and combine with the remaining oil.

3 Remove the beans from the oven and toss them with the garlic/lemon zest mixture. Return them to the oven and roast for another 5–7 minutes.

4 Remove the beans from the oven, toss them with the Parmesan cheese, and serve at once.

Spicy Szechuan Green Beans

Makes 6 servings

Pleasingly spicy and rich with umami, these green beans get their marvelous flavor and texture from both the sauce and the cooking method. Piling fresh green beans into a very hot pan and completely leaving them alone, without stirring them or moving the pan, will change the beans from snap-fresh to caramelized and slightly chewy.

FOR THE SAUCE
2½ tablespoons hoisin sauce

2 teaspoons rice vinegar

1 teaspoon sesame oil

1 tablespoon soy sauce

2 teaspoons sambal oelek

3 tablespoons peanut or vegetable oil, divided

2 pounds fresh green beans, stem ends trimmed off,
   cut into 2-inch pieces

4 ounces fresh shiitake mushrooms, stems trimmed off,
   caps sliced into ½-inch strips

1-inch piece fresh ginger root, peeled and chopped fine

2 fat garlic cloves, minced or pressed

3 green onions, ends trimmed off, thinly sliced

1 For the sauce: Mix all of the ingredients together in a small bowl and set aside.

2 For the beans: Heat 2 tablespoons of the peanut or vegetable oil in a 6-quart (or larger) pot or a large wok over medium-high to high heat (medium-high for electric stoves, high for gas stoves). When the oil starts to dimple, add the green beans, distributing them evenly across the pot. Cover the pot and allow the beans to sit undisturbed (don't stir them or shake the pot) for 2 minutes. After 2 minutes, the green beans will be bright green. Stir them, turning them with a wooden spoon or rubber spatula, to coat them all in oil. Lower the heat to medium and cook, stirring every 2 minutes, for 10–12 minutes. The green beans will develop charred bits in places, which is what you want.

3 Remove the beans to a dinner plate. Add the remaining oil to the pan and add the mushrooms, ginger, and garlic. Cook for 2 minutes, stirring constantly, until the mushrooms are soft. Return the green beans to the pot and add the sauce. Stir well, bring to a bubble (this should take a matter of seconds), then scatter the green onions over the top and stir through the beans. Serve at once.

Classic Greens

CONTEMPORARY GARLICKY KALE WITH CASHEWS

INTERNATIONAL PORTUGUESE CALDO VERDE

My conversion to greens lover occurred fifteen years ago in Augusta, Georgia. I grew up eating vegetables cooked al dente and was reluctant to try those that had been simmered for an hour (or more). But it took just one bite of those soft, savory, slightly smoky and tart greens to convert me for good.

Slowly simmered greens are a treat. Collards, mustard, or turnip greens (and sometimes Swiss chard or kale) can be used interchangeably, or mixed together. A chunk of smoked meat plays an important role for traditional greens, but for a vegetarian dish you can replace them with a few dashes of liquid smoke at the end of cooking. Vinegar is another crucial flavor element: There is a synergy between the rich, smoky, salty, and sour notes.

Don't neglect the pot likker! Full of nutrients, pot likker is the wonderful broth left behind in the pot after the greens have simmered. Dunk bread in it, drink it by the cupful, or freeze it to use later as a base for soup.

Sautéing kale quickly keeps the nutritional value high; adding garlic and rich cashews will win over the most ardent green-o-phobe.

The Portuguese Green Soup is thick because of the puréed potatoes, not added fat. Serve it with a piece of bakery bread and it's a meal.

Classic Greens

Makes 6–8
side-dish servings

If you can't find collards where you are, use kale or any other dark green (like Swiss chard, or even spinach in a pinch).

1 smoked turkey wing or thigh, 1 smoked ham hock, or
   4 ounces smoked bacon, cut into 1-inch pieces
1 medium onion, peeled and cut in half
1 tablespoon kosher or sea salt
1 large bunch collards (about 16 cups loosely packed
   chopped leaves)
2 tablespoons cider or white vinegar

All greens are exceptionally healthy, but collards are considered a superfood because of their antioxidants and reported cholesterol-lowering qualities. Some experts recommend that we eat 1½ cups steamed collards or other dark greens two to three times a week.

1 Grab the largest pot you own—a pasta pot is perfect for this. Place the smoked meat and the onions in, then pour in enough hot water to fill one-third of the pot. Add the salt and set the pot over medium-high heat. Cover the pot and bring to a simmer; crack the lid and keep the liquid at a constant, gentle simmer for 1 hour.

2 While the liquid (which will become the collards' "liquor," or "likker") is simmering, wash the collard leaves and place them on kitchen towels to drain a bit. Remove the tough stem of each leaf either by cutting it out with a knife or by holding the stem firmly with one hand and stripping the leaf away with your other hand. Stack 3–5 similar-sized leaves on top of each other and roll in either direction (lengthwise or widthwise—it really doesn't matter), so that the stack looks like a huge cigar. Slice each "collard cigar" into 1-inch strips. Continue doing this until all the leaves are chopped.

3 After the smoked meat and the onions have simmered for an hour, remove them and add the chopped collards. Stir and add enough hot water to just submerge the collards. Cover and bring to a simmer. Crack the lid and gently simmer the collards for 1 hour. While the collards are cooking, pick any meat from the wing or hock, if you can; if not, no worries—plenty of flavor was left behind in the pot likker.

4 After 1 hour of simmering, pull the collards from the pot likker (southerners like to soak up this fabulous savory liquid with bread or biscuits, and you can also use it to make the most delicious white bean soup you've ever tasted). Place the cooked collards in a large bowl (they will have wilted substantially and will have gone from deep green to a less attractive but ridiculously delicious brownish green), season with the vinegar, and toss in the bacon or any meat picked from the hock or wing. Stir well to combine. Serve at once with hot sauce on the side.

Garlicky Kale with Cashews

Makes 4–6 servings

This is a different way to sauté: You start with a cold pan. Gently warming the olive oil with the garlic ensures that the garlic cooks evenly, allowing the essential oils to really blossom without burning.

All greens (collard, mustard, turnip, kale, Swiss chard, and spinach) pack a significant nutrient wallop. This recipe retains most of the kale's nutrients because it is cooked so quickly.

> 12 cups chopped fresh kale (the leaves from ¾ of a large bunch)
> ¼ cup extra-virgin olive oil
> 3–4 fat garlic cloves, minced (about 2 tablespoons)
> ½ cup chopped roasted and salted cashews
> ½ teaspoon kosher or sea salt
> Lemon wedge

1   Remove the tough stem of each kale leaf either by cutting it out with a knife or by holding the stem firmly with one hand and stripping the leaf away with your other hand.

2   Place the olive oil and garlic in a room-temperature Dutch oven (don't preheat the pot). Set it over medium heat and allow the oil and garlic to warm slowly, for about 2 minutes. When you can smell the garlic, add the cashews and sauté them for just 1 minute, then add the kale and salt, turning the kale so that the cashews are on top. Sauté for 5 minutes, until the kale is wilted and reduced in volume. Remove the pot from the heat, squeeze the lemon over the kale, and put the lid back on. Allow the kale to rest (sit in its own residual heat) for 5 minutes before serving.

Garlicky Kale with Cashews

Portuguese Caldo Verde

Makes 8 servings

This gorgeous green soup is a meal in itself. It originated in northern Portugal but is now eaten throughout that country, especially during times of celebration (weddings, birthdays, or Christmas, for instance).

Traditionally, the sausage in this soup is simmered separately and added at the last minute, but I skipped that step, simply cooking it in the soup pot before adding the rest of the ingredients.

> 10 medium/large collard leaves or large kale leaves, finely chopped
> 3 tablespoons extra-virgin olive oil, divided
> 8 ounces Andouille, Linguica, or smoked sausage
> 1 large yellow onion, peeled and chopped fine
> 4 fat garlic cloves, thinly sliced
> 12 cups chicken broth (or pot likker)
> 4 medium/large baking potatoes, peeled and chopped into small chunks

1 Wash the greens. Remove the tough stem from each leaf either by cutting it out with a knife or by holding the stem firmly with one hand and stripping the leaf away with your other hand. Stack 5 of the collard or kale leaves (of similar size) and roll lengthwise so that the stack looks like a cigar. Thinly slice the "cigar" cross-wise (trying not to let the slices unroll), then chop the rounds into smaller pieces—they don't have to be uniform, just small. Repeat with the remaining leaves, and set aside.

2 Set a 6- to 8-quart stockpot (pasta pot) over medium heat and add 2 tablespoons of the oil. If the sausage is very firm, slice it in half lengthwise and then into half-moon pieces and add them to the pot. If the sausage is squishy, squeeze the meat from its casing into the pot. Sauté, stirring every minute or so (and if you've removed the sausage from the casing, breaking it up with a spatula as it cooks), until the sausage is just cooked through and firm, about 4 minutes. (Sausage that's been removed from its casing, may need to be cooked an additional 4 minutes.) Remove the sausage to a plate and set aside.

3 There should be 2 tablespoons of the fat in the pot. If there's more than that, take some out; if there's less, add the remaining oil. Add the onions and garlic and sauté until soft and fragrant, about 4–5 minutes. Add the chicken broth and potato chunks, turn the heat up to medium-high, and bring the soup to a simmer. Allow it to bubble away, uncovered, for 10–15 minutes, or until the potato chunks are falling apart, then use an immersion blender (or a po-tato masher, or transfer the soup to the bowl of a food processor or a stand blender) to purée the soup.

4 Once the soup is puréed to your liking (it can be smooth or lumpy), return the sausage to the pot, along with the collards or kale—don't worry, the greens collapse considerably once cooked. Stir and bring to a boil, then reduce the heat to medium and simmer, uncovered, for 10 minutes. Serve piping hot.

Classic Fried Okra

CONTEMPORARY **CRISPY COCONUT-OIL OKRA**

INTERNATIONAL **INDIAN BHINDI MASALA**

Okra, sometimes called "ladies' fingers," needs heat to grow. It's a sub-tropical and tropical plant that is found in the U.S. South and in African and Asian countries.

Southerners loyally love okra, especially fried. You may have heard that okra is slimy, and it is, but there are ways of preparing the pods that greatly reduce or eliminate the goo. I'll give you those tips in the recipes that follow.

Crispy Coconut-Oil Okra is a favorite with my children (the crunchy little spheres get snapped up in minutes), but my husband and I prefer the spicy Bhindi Masala, served tapas style among an array of Indian dishes.

Look for fresh okra in the hot summer months. The pods should be bright green, firm, and 3–4 inches long (any larger and they could be tough). Avoid pods that are limp or have brown spots.

opposite: Classic Fried Okra

Classic Fried Okra

Makes 4 servings

These crunchy fried nuggets are good even straight out of the refrigerator, cold (I know that for a fact because I've eaten them that way for breakfast). Using cornstarch instead of flour in the breading is the secret to making these beauties extra-crisp.

> 1 pound fresh okra
> 1½ cups fine cornmeal
> 1½ cups cornstarch
> 1 teaspoon onion powder
> 1 teaspoon garlic powder
> 1 cup buttermilk
> 1 egg
> 1 teaspoon hot sauce
> 1–2 cups peanut oil
> Popcorn salt

1 Slice off the stem ends off the okra, then slice the pods crosswise into 1-inch rounds. Mix the cornmeal, cornstarch, onion powder, and garlic powder in a bowl and set aside (this mixture is the "dredge"). Whisk the buttermilk, egg, and hot sauce in a separate bowl and set aside.

2 Preheat the oven to 225°. Pour enough oil into a 10-inch cast-iron or heavy skillet so that it comes 1 inch up the side, then cover the skillet and set it over medium heat. Allow the oil to reach 350–375°—this will take about 7 minutes.

3 Meanwhile, place the okra rounds in the bowl with the buttermilk and allow them to soak: The lactic acid in the buttermilk will help decrease sliminess in the okra.

4 The oil will look dimpled when it's hot. Flick a few drops of water into it; if it bubbles, it's ready. Pull about a quarter of the okra out of the buttermilk and dredge it in the cornmeal mixture, then place the okra rounds in the hot oil, one at a time. The okra should immediately bubble away in the oil. Stir the okra so that none of the rounds stick together, but if it happens, don't worry—it's not catastrophic, just not ideal. Fry the okra for 5 minutes, stirring and flipping occasionally. They will be a deep golden brown and crunchy. Using a slotted spoon, remove the okra to a wire rack, season generously with popcorn salt, and place in the warm oven while you fry the next batch. Serve hot or warm.

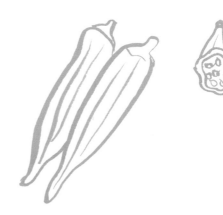

Crispy Coconut-Oil Okra

Makes 4 servings

I always find these oven-fried okra surprisingly crunchy—even without frying. Their color is not as deep and golden as their classic fried cousins', but they are equally delicious. Have your popcorn salt at the ready—it clings perfectly to the nice crunchy finished pieces.

    1 pound fresh okra
    1½ cups fine cornmeal
    1 cup panko bread crumbs
    2 teaspoons onion powder
    2 teaspoons garlic powder
    1 cup buttermilk (or milk)
    1 egg
    1 teaspoon hot sauce
    ⅓ cup melted coconut oil, divided
    Popcorn salt

1 Slice the stem ends off the okra, then slice the pods crosswise into 1-inch rounds. Mix the dredge: cornmeal, bread crumbs, onion powder, and garlic powder in a bowl and set aside. Whisk the buttermilk, egg, and hot sauce in a separate bowl and set aside.

2 Preheat the oven to 400°. Place the okra rounds in the bowl with the buttermilk and allow them to soak: The lactic acid in the buttermilk will help decrease sliminess in the okra.

3 Pour 3 tablespoons of the coconut oil into a jelly roll pan and spread evenly with a pastry brush. Remove a quarter of the okra from the buttermilk mixture and toss the pieces in the dredge, coating all sides. Place the dredged pieces on the pan, then continue with the remaining okra, a quarter at a time. Carefully drizzle 2 tablespoons of the coconut oil over the prepared okra and bake for 10 minutes. Remove the okra from the oven, stir it, drizzle the remaining coconut oil over it, and place it back in the oven for 10 minutes longer, until the pieces are crunchy. Remove from the oven and sprinkle with popcorn salt. Serve hot or warm.

Indian Bhindi Masala

Makes 4 servings

Okra is called *bhindi* in India. Cooking the okra alone, before adding spices and tomatoes, is one of the secrets to slime-free okra (some people find the slime off-putting). Beware: This dish is spicy. I love its heat alongside a simple Indian dal and basmati rice. If you want to make it milder, just back off a bit on the red pepper flakes.

1 pound fresh okra

3 tablespoons vegetable oil, divided

1 medium red onion, chopped (1 cup chopped)

2 tablespoons chopped fresh ginger root

2 tablespoons chopped garlic

1 large jalapeño pepper, trimmed, seeds removed, and finely chopped

2 cups chopped tomatoes

½ teaspoon red pepper flakes

1 teaspoon kosher or sea salt

2 teaspoons garam masala powder

1 teaspoon lime juice

Frozen okra can be used in place of fresh in this recipe, though there might be a bit of slime in the final product. Just cook the okra for an additional 5 minutes in step 1.

1 Slice the stem ends off the okra, then slice the pods crosswise into ½-inch rounds. Place a 3- to 4-quart saucepan over medium heat and add 2 tablespoons of the oil. When the oil starts to dimple, add the okra and sauté, stirring regularly, for 15 minutes, or until it's deep golden and shriveled. Remove the pan from the heat and transfer the okra to a dinner plate.

2 Place the saucepan back over medium heat and add the remaining oil. When the oil starts to dimple, add the onions, ginger, garlic, and jalapeño and sauté until soft, about 3 minutes. Add the tomatoes and their juice, red pepper flakes, salt, garam masala powder, and lime juice. Cook until the tomatoes break down and the sauce thickens, about 10 minutes. Taste the sauce and adjust seasoning with more salt or red pepper flakes, if desired. Add the okra to the tomato sauce and stir, cooking for 1 minute, just long enough to heat up the okra. Serve at once.

Indian Bhindi Masala

10

Classic Summer Squash Casserole

CONTEMPORARY **GOAT CHEESE AND THYME SQUASH CASSEROLE**

INTERNATIONAL **CRUNCHY ITALIAN ZUCCHINI WEDGES**

Zucchini and yellow squash are probably the most popular and easy-to-find summer squash. Botanically, they are actually fruit, but they are treated as a savory vegetable by most home cooks. They are picked when immature, when their skin is not yet tough (as with winter squash, such as pumpkin or butternut), so the entire vegetable can be eaten: skin, flesh, seeds, flowers, shoots, and all. I think of summer squash as the tofu of the vegetable world—its flavor is mild, making it the perfect canvas for seasonings and layers of flavors.

Summer squash casserole is an absolute mainstay on southern tables in the warmer months. People seem to grow zucchini and yellow squash whether they like squash or not, and turning it into a creamy, cheesy, comforting casserole makes tending to that garden worthwhile. As good as the classic summer squash casserole is, I prefer the healthier version, with its delicate flavors, like goat cheese and fresh thyme. And it's hard to resist the crunchy Italian zucchini wedges!—fun because you can eat them with your hands, but oh so delicious, too.

Classic Summer Squash Casserole

Makes 6–8 servings

I use both yellow squash and zucchini in this recipe—I think the dish is prettier that way. Look for firm zucchini and yellow squash, with bright color and no soft or brown spots.

This southern summer staple is a really easy dish to prepare and great to bring to a gathering.

5 tablespoons butter, divided

3 medium yellow squash

3 medium zucchini

1 large Vidalia onion, chopped

2 large garlic cloves, minced or pressed

1½ teaspoons kosher or sea salt, divided

1½ cups crushed Ritz crackers (about 36 crackers)

½ cup freshly grated Parmesan cheese

¼ teaspoon garlic powder

8 ounces sour cream

2 tablespoons all-purpose flour

1 cup shredded sharp cheddar cheese

1 Preheat the oven to 375°. Grease a 9 × 11-inch baking dish with 1 tablespoon of the butter (or spray with nonstick cooking spray) and set aside. Trim off both the ends of the squash and zucchini, cut them in half lengthwise, then cut each half in half lengthwise, and finally, cut each piece into quarter-moons. Melt 2 tablespoons of the butter in a 4- to 5-quart pot or Dutch oven over medium heat. When the butter is frothy, add the squash, zucchini, onions, and garlic. Sprinkle with ½ teaspoon of the salt, stir to mix the vegetables with the butter and the salt, and cover. Cook, stirring every 3–4 minutes, for 15 minutes, until the vegetables soften and lose their bright color. This method steams the vegetables in their own juices rather than water, making the final result tastier.

2 While the vegetables are cooking, in a small bowl, combine the crackers, Parmesan cheese, and garlic powder; melt the remaining butter, drizzle it over the cracker mixture, and toss to coat. Set aside.

3 Transfer the cooked vegetables to a large bowl using a slotted spoon, allowing them to drain as you lift them from the pot. Cool for 5 minutes, then add the remaining salt, the sour cream, and the flour. Stir well, add the cheddar cheese, and stir again.

4 Pour the vegetable mixture into the prepared dish and spread it out evenly. Scatter the cracker mixture over the top and bake for 20–30 minutes, or until the crackers are golden and the casserole edges are bubbly.

Goat Cheese and Thyme Squash Casserole

Makes 12 servings

Creamy, tart goat cheese mingles with fresh, herbaceous thyme in this fabulous version of a summer squash casserole. Chèvre is a wonderfully delicate type of goat cheese that imparts a subtle, creamy, slightly tangy note to this dish.

A trick to making vegetable casseroles thicker and smoother without adding heavy cream, a roux, or mayonnaise is to purée some of the cooked vegetables and mix them back in before baking.

> 3 medium yellow squash
> 3 medium zucchini
> 3 tablespoons coconut oil, divided
> 1 medium sweet onion (like Vidalia), chopped
> 3 fat garlic cloves, minced
> 5 large kale leaves, chopped (about 6 cups)
> 2 cups lima beans (1 box frozen)
> 1 teaspoon kosher or sea salt, divided
> 1 heaping teaspoon fresh thyme leaves
> 2 eggs
> 2 tablespoons all-purpose flour
> 4 ounces chèvre (spreadable goat cheese)
> 1½ cups crushed Ritz crackers (about 36 crackers)

1 Trim off both ends of the squash and the zucchini, cut them in half lengthwise, then cut each half in half lengthwise, and finally, cut each piece into quarter-moons.

2 Preheat the oven to 375°. Spray a 9 ×11-inch baking dish with nonstick cooking spray and set aside. Melt 2 tablespoons of the coconut oil in a lidded 4- or 5-quart pot over medium heat. When the oil starts to dimple, add the squash, zucchini, onions, garlic, kale, and lima beans. Sprinkle with ½ teaspoon of the salt, stir to mix the vegetables with the oil and salt, then cover. Cook, stirring every 3–4 minutes, for 15 minutes, or until the vegetables soften and lose their bright color. This method steams the vegetables in their own juices rather than water, making the final result tastier.

3 While the vegetables are cooking, whisk the thyme, eggs, and flour together in a small bowl. Set aside.

4 Transfer the cooked vegetables from their cooking pot to a large bowl using a slotted spoon, allowing them to drain as you lift them from the pot. Place half of the cooked vegetables in the bowl of a food processor with the chèvre and the remaining salt. Purée until smooth (a few lumps will remain). Return the puréed vegetable/chèvre mixture to the bowl with the other vegetables and stir. Allow the mixture to cool to room temperature, then add the egg mixture, stirring to distribute it evenly.

5 Pour the vegetable mixture into the prepared dish, spreading it out evenly. Scatter the cracker crumbs over the top, melt the remaining coconut oil and drizzle it over the crumbs. Cover with foil and bake for 30 minutes; remove the foil and bake 15–30 minutes longer, or until the crackers are golden and the casserole edges are bubbly.

Crunchy Italian Zucchini Wedges

Makes 4–6 servings

These spicy, crunchy wedges are absolutely addictive! No sauce needed to drizzle or dunk—the crust is crisp and full of flavor and the zucchini within bakes up ultra-soft—the perfect foil to the spicy exterior. Make more than you think you will eat. Trust me: These fly off the table.

1 tablespoon coconut, vegetable, or olive oil

2 large or 3 medium zucchini

1 cup all-purpose flour

3 eggs

1 cup freshly grated Parmesan cheese

1 cup panko bread crumbs

1 teaspoon onion powder

1 teaspoon garlic powder

1 teaspoon red pepper flakes (or less for delicate palates)

1 teaspoon kosher or sea salt

2 teaspoons Italian seasoning

1 Preheat the oven to 425°. Using a paper towel, grease a sheet pan with the coconut, vegetable, or olive oil. Trim off both ends of the zucchini, then cut each zucchini in half lengthwise. Cut each half lengthwise again into ½-inch thick wedges, then cut the wedges into 3-inch-long segments (you should get 16 wedges from a large zucchini, 12 wedges from a medium). Set aside.

2 Set up the breading station: In a pie plate, place the flour. In a second pie plate, lightly beat the eggs. In a third pie plate, mix together the Parmesan, bread crumbs, onion powder, garlic powder, red pepper flakes, salt, and Italian seasoning.

3 Working in batches of 4–6 wedges at a time, toss them in the flour, shake off the excess, coat them in the eggs (use a fork to help turn them over in the eggs) and then in the Parmesan/panko (shaking off any excess), and put them on the prepared pan in a single layer (don't let them overlap at all). This classic three-step coating will seal in the zucchini as it bakes, so that it steams in its own juices but the crust bakes up crunchy, light, and delicious.

4 Bake for 15 minutes, then flip the wedges over and continue baking for 10–15 minutes longer, or until golden. Serve hot.

11

Classic Tomato Pie

CONTEMPORARY **TOMATO PIE WITH QUINOA CRUST**

INTERNATIONAL **PROVENÇAL TOMATO TART**

When we lived in Augusta, Georgia, the presence of a tomato pie on a lunch or dinner table was a sure sign that summer had arrived. Throughout the South, 'mater pie, with its juicy red interior and rich, cheesy top, is an addition to meals of all sorts: weeknight family meals, casual gatherings with friends, or large, social picnics.

Giving the classic tomato pie a twist by using a quinoa crust makes this already delicious southern mainstay a hearty meal unto itself.

Flipping the traditional recipe once more by incorporating flavors of Provence emphasizes the versatility of ripe summer tomatoes.

Classic Tomato Pie

This simple, sublime dish really pulls together all that is special about the warmer seasons, not only in the South but across the United States—it's like sunshine in a pie shell.

The key to light and flaky piecrust is using very cold fat (butter and shortening or lard) and being careful not to overwork (overmix) the dough. Note: This recipe makes enough dough for two open-top pies, so reserve half for another purpose. The dough works just as well for dessert pies as it does for savory.

It's critical to prebake the pie shell so that your tomato pie's crust doesn't end up soggy (from all those gloriously juicy tomatoes). If you don't care for sharp cheddar, use mild cheddar or even shredded mozzarella.

If you are in a pinch for time, store-bought prerolled pie dough, found in the refrigerated section, will work.

FOR THE CRUST

2½ cups sifted all-purpose flour (sift before measuring)

1 teaspoon kosher or sea salt

1 teaspoon granulated sugar

1½ sticks butter, cut into cubes and refrigerated
   until very cold

½ cup (8 tablespoons) vegetable shortening or lard,
   refrigerated until very cold

6–8 tablespoons ice water

3 tablespoons all-purpose flour (for rolling)

2 cups dried beans or uncooked rice (for baking the crust)

½ cup freshly grated Parmesan or Pecorino cheese

FOR THE FILLING

1½ pounds ripe tomatoes

1 teaspoon kosher or sea salt flakes

1 cup mayonnaise

1 cup shredded cheddar cheese (mild, sharp, or extra-sharp)

¼ teaspoon freshly cracked black pepper

1 cup thinly sliced sweet onion (like Vidalia) (about half of
a small onion)

1 For the crust: Mix the flour, salt, and sugar in a food processor
using the "pulse" mode, just a few times. Add the butter and pulse
3–6 times (for 1-second intervals). Add the shortening in eight
1-tablespoon pieces and pulse again, 3–6 times, until the mixture
looks like coarse cornmeal, with just a few pea-sized fat lumps
remaining.

2 One tablespoon at a time, sprinkle in 6 tablespoons of the ice
water (just the water, not the ice), pulsing after each addition,
just to combine. (The dough will not pull together at this point.)
Be careful not to overmix. Take a bit of dough and squeeze it
between your fingers. If it holds together, you've added enough
water; if it crumbles apart, add more water, one teaspoon at a time,
until the dough holds together when squeezed.

3 Turn the dough out onto a clean countertop, divide it in half, and
form each half into a ball. Don't knead more than you have to just
to pull the dough into a rough ball shape. Squish each ball down
into a disk shape about ¾ inch thick and wrap separately in plastic
wrap. Refrigerate for at least 1 hour. (The dough will keep in the
refrigerator for up to 2 days.) Remove the dough from the refrigerator 10 minutes before rolling.

4 Preheat the oven to 400°. Sprinkle the flour onto a clean work surface. Roll the dough into a 14-inch round about ¼ inch thick. Fold
the dough loosely in half to transfer it to an ungreased 9-inch pie
dish; with the seam in the middle, unfold the dough so that it covers the dish. Lightly press the dough against the sides and bottom
of the dish, being careful not to stretch it. Trim and discard any
dough hanging over the edge.

5 Using a fork, prick the dough all over about two dozen times (this is called docking and will help keep the dough from puffing up as it bakes). Lay a sheet of parchment paper or foil on top of the pie dough and push it to fit into the shape of the dish. Pour in the dried beans or uncooked rice, making sure they fill the dish evenly.

6 Bake the crust for 20 minutes, remove it from the oven, and lift out the parchment paper or foil with the beans/rice (they can be composted or used again). Sprinkle the Parmesan or Pecorino cheese over the bottom of the crust, place it back in the oven, and bake it for 5 minutes longer. Remove it from the oven. You will see that the cheese has melted into the crust and that the crust is golden in some areas, but mostly the same color as raw dough. Allow the crust to cool completely. Reduce the oven temperature to 350°.

7 For the filling: While the crust is baking, slice the tomatoes in half around their equator and gently squeeze the seeds out (discard or compost them). Slice the tomato halves into ½-inch slices. Line a jelly roll pan or several dinner plates with paper towels and lay the tomato slices on top, then sprinkle them evenly with the salt. Allow the tomatoes to sit for 10–15 minutes: The salt will draw the liquid from them, and the paper towels will soak it up.

8 In a small bowl, mix together the mayonnaise, cheddar cheese, and pepper and set aside.

9 When the crust is room temperature, layer half of the tomatoes on the bottom, followed by all of the sliced onions, then the remaining tomatoes.

10 Dollop the mayo/cheese mixture into the center of the pie, on top of the tomatoes, and gently spread it outward, until you get almost to the crust. Bake for 40–45 minutes, or until the cheese is slightly golden. (Check after 25 minutes of baking time to see if the crust is too golden. You may need to cover the pie loosely with a piece of foil as it continues to bake to prevent the crust from becoming too dark.) Remove the pie from the oven and allow it to cool for at least 20 minutes before slicing. Serve warm, room temperature, or chilled.

Tomato Pie with Quinoa Crust

The quinoa and the Parmesan bake up into a crunchy, hearty crust. It also adds heart-healthy and gluten-free elements to this tomato pie. Replacing half of the cheddar with the Parmesan or Pecorino cheese substantially lowers the fat but still gives the pie a solid cheesy flavor.

Makes one 9-inch pie

Quinoa is a seed, indigenous to South America. It's high in protein and gluten free. It's very important to cook quinoa in a flavorful liquid, even if that flavor is only salted water. Vegetable, chicken, or beef broth works well too. Allow at least 15 minutes to soak the quinoa before making the crust—this is an important step, not to be skipped.

FOR THE CRUST
¾ cup quinoa
1 cup flavorful liquid (like vegetable, chicken, or beef broth)
½ cup freshly grated Parmesan or Pecorino cheese
2 eggs, beaten

FOR THE FILLING

½ cup plain Greek yogurt

½ cup mayonnaise (light or regular)

½ cup shredded extra-sharp reduced-fat cheddar cheese

1½ pounds ripe tomatoes, cut into ½-inch slices

1 cup thinly sliced sweet onion (like Vidalia)
   (about ½ small onion)

½ cup freshly grated Parmesan or Pecorino cheese

Kosher or sea salt, to taste

1 For the crust: Place the quinoa in a bowl and cover with water by 1 inch. Soak for 15 minutes. Drain well in a mesh sieve.

2 Place the quinoa in a small pot and add the flavorful liquid. Cover and set over medium-high heat. Watch closely, and as soon as steam comes out of the pot and the liquid is simmering strongly, reduce the heat to the lowest setting and allow the quinoa to cook, covered, very gently until all of the water is absorbed, about 15–25 minutes.

3 Preheat the oven to 375°. Spray a 9-inch pie pan with nonstick cooking spray. Combine the quinoa, Parmesan or Pecorino cheese, and eggs until well mixed and place the mixture into the middle of the pan. Press the mixture along the bottom and up the sides of the pan so that it's of equal thickness on the bottom and sides— it should be about ¼–½ inch thick.

4 Bake for 30 minutes, or until slightly golden in spots. Allow the crust to cool to room temperature before adding the filling.

5 For the filling: In a small bowl, mix together the yogurt, mayonnaise, and cheddar cheese. When the crust is room temperature, layer half of the tomatoes on the bottom, followed by all of the sliced onions, then the remaining tomatoes. Dollop the yogurt mixture in the center of the pie and gently spread it outward until you get almost to the crust.

6 Bake for 35–45 minutes, or until the cheese is slightly golden.

Provençal Tomato Tart

Makes about twelve
3-by-3-inch slices

The term "Provençal" in this recipe indicates that it's of the style of Provence. Located in southeastern France, Provence is a region that rolls from the west and the lower Rhone River east to Italy and south to the Mediterranean Sea.

My aunt Gretchen and uncle David own a home there and were kind enough to invite our large, unwieldy family of six to visit one spring. We piled into the minivan and barreled south from our home in Zürich, around and through the Alps, across the top of Italy, and finally along the cliffside drive into the South of France. The French Riviera was so blue and clear that I came to understand why it was named the Côte d'Azur, or Blue Coast.

My aunt was an incredible cook, influenced by her surroundings in Provence but even more so by her mother, my grandmother, who was the ultimate midwestern scratch-cook.

Uncle David met us at the door, as Gretchen had dinner just coming out of the oven: tomato, goat cheese, and black olive tart, followed by duck braised with apricots and green olives, washed down with a chilled, crisp rosé. The very few ingredients in each dish were all exceptionally fresh and flavorful. Even our three-year-old twins seemed to recognize the beauty of that meal—the wonderful culmination of food and family.

Two 9½ × 9½-inch sheets store-bought frozen puff pastry (thawed according to package directions)
1½ pounds ripe tomatoes
1 teaspoon kosher or sea salt
1 (5.3-ounce) log soft, spreadable goat cheese
½–1 teaspoon freshly cracked black pepper
6 sprigs fresh thyme
4 fat garlic cloves, thinly sliced
18 oil-cured black olives

1 Preheat the oven to 400°. Unroll the puff pastry sheets and place them on an ungreased jelly roll pan end to end, so that they make a 19-inch-long sheet. Press the seam between the two sheets well to join them together. Cut off 2–3 inches of pastry so that the sheet fits into the pan. Using a fork, prick the dough all over about two dozen times (this is called docking and will help keep the dough from puffing up as it bakes). Bake for 10 minutes, remove it from the oven, and allow it to cool completely. It will have started to puff up in places, but that's fine. Keep the oven temperature at 400°.

2 While the pastry is baking, slice the tomatoes in half around their equator and gently squeeze the seeds out (discard or compost them). Slice the tomato halves into ½-inch slices. Line a sheet pan or several dinner plates with paper towels and lay the tomato slices on top, then sprinkle evenly with the salt. Allow the tomatoes to sit for 10–15 minutes: The salt will draw the liquid from them, and the paper towels will soak it up.

3 Meanwhile, strip the leaves from the thyme sprig by either pulling them off individually or running your fingers backward down the stem to rip them off. When the pastry is room temperature, spread the goat cheese evenly across the pastry, then sprinkle with the pepper and scatter the garlic slices evenly across the cheese. Layer the tomatoes on top, overlapping them a bit, and finish with the thyme leaves. Scatter the olives across the tart evenly and bake it for 20–30 minutes, or until the crust is golden. Allow the tart to cool for 5–10 minutes before cutting.

12

Classic Creamy Coleslaw

CONTEMPORARY **CRUNCHY DILL SLAW**

INTERNATIONAL **MEXICAN SLAW**

Fresh cabbage is at the heart of every coleslaw (*Kohl* is the German word for cabbage) and is what gives coleslaw its crunch. Even when made a whole day ahead, coleslaw retains most of its crisp texture. The flavor combinations are practically endless, too: creamy mayo-based dressing, sharp vinaigrette, or maybe buttermilk, mixed with any number of types of cabbage and assorted vegetables and sometimes fruit (like apples or raisins). In Italy they even add ham strips to their slaw. In Lexington, North Carolina, they serve up "red slaw," in which ketchup replaces the mayonnaise in the dressing and which is a ubiquitous side to that region's amazing barbecue.

From the humble cabbage can come some marvelous salads that use ingredients from all over the globe.

Classic Creamy Coleslaw

*Makes 8–12
side-dish servings*

This is a great example of when crunchy and creamy collide into a gorgeously simple side dish. Sweet and tangy, this salad pairs perfectly with barbecue—which in the South is a noun, not a verb, and in some parts of the South only means slowly cooked pork.

½ cup mayonnaise

3 tablespoons granulated sugar

1 tablespoon white vinegar

1 teaspoon kosher or sea salt

½ teaspoon freshly cracked black pepper

½ large head green cabbage (about 1 pound)

½ large head purple cabbage (about 1 pound)

1 large carrot, peeled

1 bunch green onions, trimmed and sliced (using the entire onion, white to dark green)

1 In a medium bowl, mix the mayonnaise, sugar, vinegar, salt, and pepper together using a wire whisk or table fork until they are well combined. Set aside.

2 Cut each cabbage in half, then cut out the core and cut the cabbages in half again so that the pieces are easy to hold in your hand. Slice each cabbage quarter very thinly, as thin as you can manage. If you have a mandoline and are confident with it, this is a great recipe for which to use it; you can also use the large holes of a box grater. Pile the cabbage in a large bowl. You will have about 10 cups (which decreases in volume once dressed). Shred the carrot on the large holes of a box grater.

3 Pile the cabbage in a large bowl, add the carrots and onions, then toss with the dressing. Cover and store in the refrigerator until ready to serve (up to 24 hours).

Crunchy Dill Coleslaw

🍴

Makes 8 servings

Crisp fresh celery adds an additional crunch to this slaw. Lemon juice and dill keep the flavor light and refreshing. If you can get your hands on high-quality sherry vinegar, snap it up—its flavor is slightly less acidic and more refined than white or even cider vinegars. I find myself craving this slaw if I go too long without it.

1 tablespoon lemon juice

¼ cup sherry or apple cider vinegar

1 teaspoon kosher or sea salt

1 tablespoon dried dill weed

½ cup light olive or vegetable oil

½ head green cabbage (about 1 pound)

½ head purple cabbage (about 1 pound)

2–3 celery stalks, chopped

1 bunch green onions, trimmed and sliced
(using the entire onion, white to dark green)

1 In a medium bowl, mix the lemon juice, vinegar, salt, and dill weed together using a wire whisk or table fork until the salt dissolves, then whisk in the oil. Set aside.

2 Cut each cabbage in half, then cut out the core and cut the cabbages in half again so that the pieces are easy to hold in your hand. Slice each cabbage quarter very thinly, as thin as you can manage. If you have a mandoline and are confident with it, this is a great recipe for which to use it; you can also use the large holes of a box grater.

3 Pile the cabbage in a large bowl, add the celery and onions, then toss with the dressing. Serve at once or store in the refrigerator for up to 3 days.

Mexican Slaw

Makes 8 servings

Crisp cabbage dressed in a lime- and honey-infused vinaigrette keeps its fresh crunch, while the jalapeño adds just the right amount of bite. If you can make classic coleslaw, then you can definitely make Mexican coleslaw. Don't forgo the fish sauce; in this recipe as in so many others, fish sauce adds a salty zing without the slightest trace of fish.

¼ cup lime juice

1½ teaspoons kosher or sea salt

¼ cup honey or agave nectar

Zest of ½ lime

1 teaspoon ground cumin

1 teaspoon fish sauce (don't skip this)

2 tablespoons olive oil

½ cup chopped fresh cilantro

2 tablespoons finely minced jalapeño

½ large head green cabbage (about 1 pound)

½ large head purple cabbage (about 1 pound)

8 ounces radishes, both ends trimmed

1 bunch green onions, trimmed and sliced (using the entire onion, white to dark green)

1 In a medium bowl, mix the lime juice and salt together using
   a wire whisk or table fork until the salt dissolves, then add the
   honey or agave and whisk until well distributed. Whisk in the lime
   zest, cumin, and fish sauce, then the oil, and finally the cilantro and
   jalapeño. It will have the consistency of vinaigrette. Set aside.
2 Cut each cabbage in half, then cut out the core and cut the
   cabbage in half again so that the pieces are easy to hold in your
   hand. Slice each cabbage quarter very thinly, as thin as you can
   manage. If you have a mandoline and are confident with it, this
   is a great recipe for which to use it; you can also use the large
   holes of a box grater. Slice the radishes, then cut the slices into
   matchstick-sized pieces.
3 Pile the cabbage in a large bowl, add the radishes and onions,
   and toss with the dressing. Serve at once or store in the refrigerator for up to 3 days.

13

Classic Macaroni and Cheese

CONTEMPORARY **THREE-CHEESE MACARONI WITH PURÉED BUTTERNUT SQUASH**

INTERNATIONAL **SWISS ÄLPLERMAGRONEN**

Soft, tender noodles intertwined with meltingly rich cheese is the stuff of dreams (at least for me). Add a layer of crispy crumb topping and you've conjured up possibly one of the best dishes ever. On earth. I mean it.

"Mac and cheese" means something different depending on whom you're talking to. For some people, its most familiar form comes from a box containing a packet of powdered cheese. Full disclosure: My children *love* this kind of mac and cheese. For others, it's a scratch-made dish: a creamy, roux-thickened cheese sauce splashed over a pile of cooked noodles. For most southerners, it's baked with a crunchy crumb topping. It's on every holiday table, at every family gathering, wake, and barbecue. The southern citizen's contract seems to have this unwritten clause: Wherever there is a group of people gathered, there *will* be baked mac and cheese.

I developed the recipe for the Three-Cheese Macaroni and Cheese with Puréed Butternut Squash when we were expats living in Zürich. My children had grown fond of baked macaroni and cheese when we lived in Augusta, Georgia, and because one recipe would make enough dinners for days, it was well worth the effort. I wanted to figure out how to make this most beloved of dishes healthier. Adding a gorgeous pop of nutritionally supercharged orange butternut squash worked magic. Using stronger cheeses added more flavor while reducing fat—it was a win/win.

It was also while living in Switzerland that our family discovered Älplermagronen, the Alpine style of macaroni and cheese. It's much milder than classic macaroni and cheese, but absolutely delicious, thanks in part to the caramelized onions and aged Gruyère.

Classic Macaroni and Cheese

Makes 12 servings

In this dish the initial crunch from the crumb topping gives way to melted cheese and wonderfully squishy noodles. This recipe uses a part-custard, part-roux-based sauce, resulting in a creamy baked casserole with pockets of gooey cheese. My beloved Velveeta is critical to the smooth melt factor, smoked Gouda brings a creamy flavor that is delicious yet indefinable, and cheddar adds a subtle sharpness. Combining the three cheeses is my secret to making an outstanding macaroni and cheese.

Be careful not to overcook the macaroni—8 minutes of hard boil time is all you need, because the noodles will cook more in the oven.

1 tablespoon kosher or sea salt

1 pound macaroni, uncooked

3½ tablespoons butter, divided

1 cup half-and-half

1 cup milk

2 eggs

1 teaspoon seasoned salt (like Lawry's brand)

⅛ teaspoon freshly cracked black pepper

½ teaspoon garlic powder

1 teaspoon Dijon mustard

1 tablespoon all-purpose flour

2 cups shredded sharp cheddar cheese

1 cup shredded smoked Gouda cheese

8 ounces Velveeta cheese, cubed

1 cup panko bread crumbs

1 Fill a large (8-quart works great) stockpot three-quarters full with hot water and add the salt. Cover and set over high heat. When the water comes to a rolling boil, add the pasta and bring it back to a boil. Boil the pasta for 8 minutes, stirring often. Drain the pasta well and toss it with 2 tablespoons of the butter. Stir the pasta every few minutes so that it cools evenly.

2 Meanwhile, use a wire whisk to blend the half-and-half, milk, eggs, seasoned salt, pepper, garlic powder, mustard, and flour. Stir in the shredded and cubed cheeses. Set aside.

3 Spray a 9 × 11-inch or 3-quart baking dish with nonstick cooking spray. After the pasta has cooled at room temperature for 10 minutes, combine it with the milk/cheese mixture, then put it all in the prepared baking dish.

4 Melt the remaining butter and combine it with the bread crumbs in a small bowl; sprinkle the bread crumb mixture evenly over the top of the macaroni and cheese. Bake, uncovered, until the top is golden, about 45 minutes. Allow to rest for 10 minutes before serving.

Classic Macaroni and Cheese

Three-Cheese Macaroni with Puréed Butternut Squash

Makes 8 main-course servings or 12 side-dish servings

The key to making I-can't-believe-this-is-healthier macaroni and cheese is twofold: Add healthy ingredients like butternut squash and coconut oil, and replace ample amounts of mild cheese with smaller amounts of strong cheeses (blue, for instance). Even if you don't care for blue cheese, use it in this recipe—it isn't pronounced but adds a real depth of flavor.

1 small butternut squash
1 pound elbow macaroni, uncooked
1 tablespoon coconut or vegetable oil
2 cups milk
¼ cup IPA or Pilsner beer
1½ teaspoons kosher or sea salt
1 tablespoon Dijon mustard
½ cup freshly grated Parmesan cheese
½ cup crumbled blue cheese
2 cups shredded extra-sharp cheddar cheese
1 cup panko bread crumbs
1½ tablespoons melted coconut oil

1 Preheat the oven to 375°. Slice the butternut squash in half (from end to end), scoop out seeds and discard. Wrap the squash in foil and roast for 1 hour, or until completely soft. Scoop the squash pulp out of the skin (and discard the skin). You should have roughly 2½ cups of cooked squash. If you want, you can do this step a day ahead and store the squash in a covered container in the refrigerator until ready to use.

2 Fill a large (8-quart works great) stockpot three-quarters full with hot water and add the salt. Cover and set over high heat. When the water comes to a rolling boil, add the pasta, cover, and bring back to a boil. Boil the pasta for 8 minutes, stirring often. Drain the pasta well, put it in a large mixing bowl, and toss it with the tablespoon of coconut or vegetable oil. Set aside.

3 Place the squash and 1 cup of the milk in the bowl of a food processor or the blender. Purée until smooth.

4 Pour the squash/milk mixture into a medium-sized pot and add the remaining milk and the beer. Bring to a simmer, stirring frequently. Add the salt and mustard, stir to blend. Remove the pot from the heat and add the cheese. Stir until the cheese has melted. Taste it and adjust the seasoning—it should taste very flavorful and fairly salty.

5 Pour the sauce over the pasta and stir well. It will be rather soupy at this point, but the pasta will absorb all of the sauce when baked.

6 Spray a 9 × 11-inch or 3-quart baking dish with nonstick cooking spray and pile the prepared pasta in it. Place the bread crumbs in a small bowl and combine them with the 1½ tablespoons of melted coconut oil; sprinkle the bread crumb mixture evenly over top of the macaroni and cheese. Bake, uncovered, until the top is golden, about 45 minutes. Allow it to rest for 10 minutes before serving.

Swiss Älplermagronen

Makes 6–8 servings

Warm and creamy, this dish is classic Swiss comfort food. When we lived in Switzerland, our two older daughters took ski lessons every Saturday at a local mountain near our home. Most of the other kids in their elementary school did too. The parents would gather at the bottom of the mountain, chatting or pulling children too young to ski on sleds. At lunchtime everyone—ski students, little siblings, and parents—would pile into a cozy ski chalet restaurant and order plates of Älplermagronen with applesauce.

> 3 tablespoons butter, divided
> 2 medium yellow onions, peeled, halved, and sliced into
>   thin half-moons (about 4 cups)
> 1 tablespoon plus 1 teaspoon kosher or sea salt, divided
> 12 ounces ziti or any straight, tubular pasta
> 2 large yellow or red waxy potatoes, cut into 1-inch cubes
> ½ teaspoon freshly cracked black pepper
> Big pinch of nutmeg
> 2 cups shredded Gruyère or Appenzeller cheese
> ½ cup heavy cream

1 Butter a 9 × 11-inch or 3-quart baking dish with 1 tablespoon of the butter and set aside. Set a cast-iron skillet or large sauté pan over medium-high heat and add the remaining butter. Once the butter froths and the frothing subsides, add the onions, sprinkle with ½ teaspoon of the salt, and stir. Lower the heat to medium or medium-low and cook, stirring every 2–3 minutes, until the onions turn golden brown and are caramelized, 25–30 minutes.

2 Preheat the oven to 375°. While the onions are deliciously cara-melizing, cook the pasta and potatoes: Fill a large (8-quart works great) stockpot three-quarters full with hot water and add 1 table-spoon of the salt. Cover and set over high heat. When the water comes to a rolling boil, add the pasta, cover, and bring back to a boil. Lower the heat to medium and boil, uncovered, for 5 min-utes, stirring twice. Add the potatoes, bring back to a boil, and cook for 8 minutes. Drain well, transfer to a large bowl, and toss with the remaining salt, the pepper, and the nutmeg.

3 Spoon a third of the hot pasta/potato mixture into the bottom of the prepared baking dish, followed by half of the cheese, then a third of the pasta/potato, then the other half of the cheese, and finally the remaining pasta/potato. Top with the caramelized onions and drizzle the heavy cream evenly over the top. Bake, uncovered, for 15 minutes. It will be a creamy, off-white color. Serve at once.

14

Classic Cheese Grits

CONTEMPORARY **SPICY SLIM GRITS WITH PECORINO AND PARMESAN**

INTERNATIONAL **NORTHERN ITALIAN POLENTA E GORGONZOLA**

A steaming bowl of creamy grits is the ultimate stick-to-your-ribs dish. Although grits have made huge inroads on restaurant dinner menus across the country, in the South they will always be a most beloved breakfast staple. They're a simple food that fill the stomach and satisfy the soul. Grits are dried corn that has been ground to the desired consistency. Most grits are white or yellow, although Anson Mills in Charleston, South Carolina, sells blue corn grits. Cornmeal and grits have been grown, ground, and eaten by Native Americans all over this country for millennia.

Grits and their Italian sister dish, polenta, are similar: Both are dried ground corn cooked with an abundance of liquid to form a porridge. The differences are found in the type of corn used to make each and the number of passes the dried corn gets through the mill. In a pinch, coarsely ground cornmeal can be used interchangeably in grits and polenta recipes.

Replacing cheddar cheese with Parmesan and Pecorino cheeses reduces fat by a lot, yet keeps a bold flavor. Taking it one step further, Italian Polenta e Gorgonzola calls for that lush blue-veined cheese (personally, I'm addicted to it): It wallops the taste buds with salty, very slightly acidic notes, then comforts with the creamy cornmeal.

All three grits recipes are naturally gluten-free and make a nice side-dish option for people with gluten intolerance.

opposite: Classic Cheese Grits

Classic Cheese Grits

Makes 6 servings

Charleston, South Carolina, is one of the most beautiful cities in the United States. You'd be hard-pressed to find someone who didn't agree. Gorgeous pastel-hued houses, warm sea breezes—it has an air of the Caribbean. And the food scene is spectacular. If you have a chance to go to that historic city, do it.

Charlestonians are known for their love of grits. Unfussy plates of shrimp and grits are served in restaurants and in private homes. Grits are most often made with water, but Charleston cooks tend to use milk, making the dish creamier. I like to use both water and milk, with a decadent finish of heavy cream.

2 cups water

2 cups whole, 2%, or 1% milk (not skim)

1 teaspoon kosher or sea salt

2 dashes cayenne pepper

¼ cup heavy cream

1 cup grits, preferably stone-ground (not quick-cooking grits)

1 cup shredded sharp (or extra-sharp) cheddar cheese

1 In a large saucepan, bring the water, milk, salt, and cayenne to a boil over medium-high heat. Remove the heavy cream from the refrigerator, to warm slightly, as you cook the grits.

2 Add the grits in a slow, steady stream, stirring them into the liquid as you do so with either a wire whisk or a wooden spoon. Lower the heat to medium-low or low and whisk or stir constantly for 2 minutes (this will prevent lumps). Continue to cook, uncovered, stirring every few minutes with a spoon. The grits should be moving, with a few little bubbles breaking at the surface, but not quite simmering. Cook until grits are thick, soft, and creamy, about 35 minutes.

3 Remove from the heat and stir in the cream (the grits will be as hot as molten lava at this point, so be careful). Immediately add the cheese and stir until the cheese has melted and the grits are lovely, creamy, and gooey. Serve at once.

Spicy Slim Grits with Pecorino and Parmesan

🍴

Makes 6 servings

For this recipe, I've substantially reduced the amount of fat in Classic Cheese Grits by getting rid of the heavy cream and cheddar cheese. To replace the lush flavor that fat adds, I've used savory chicken broth and bold notes like fresh garlic, strong (lower-fat) Pecorino and Parmesan cheese, plus two types of pepper for a spicy kick.

4½ cups chicken broth
2 garlic cloves, minced
1 cup stone-ground grits (not quick-cooking grits)
1 teaspoon freshly cracked black pepper
½ teaspoon red pepper flakes
1 tablespoon coconut oil
¼ cup grated Pecorino cheese
¼ cup grated Parmesan cheese

1 In a large saucepan, bring the chicken broth and garlic to a boil over medium-high heat.

2 Add the grits in a slow, steady stream, stirring them into the liquid as you do so with either a wire whisk or a wooden spoon. Lower the heat to medium-low or low and whisk or stir constantly for 2 minutes (this will prevent lumps). Continue to cook, uncovered, stirring every few minutes with a spoon. The grits should be moving, with a few little bubbles breaking at the surface, but not quite simmering. Cook until grits are thick, soft, and creamy, about 35 minutes.

3 Remove from the heat and stir in the black pepper, red pepper flakes, coconut oil, and cheese until meltingly delicious. Serve at once.

Spicy Slim Grits with Pecorino and Parmesan

Northern Italian Polenta e Gorgonzola

Makes 6 servings

I first tasted Polenta e Gorgonzola when our family took a long week-end trip to Ticino, the Italian region of Switzerland. Although it lies inside the Swiss borders, Ticino is Italian in language, culture, and food. Eating this dish there was a revelation: I realized immediately that it was the Italian version of cheese grits!

I've made one untraditional addition to this dish—toasted walnuts. Pairing walnuts with any blue-veined cheese is a match made in heaven, but if you don't like walnuts, you can skip them.

1 cup walnuts
4 cups water
½ teaspoon kosher or sea salt
1 cup stone-ground grits (not quick-cooking grits)
½ cup heavy cream
½ cup crumbled Gorgonzola cheese

Gorgonzola cheese is made from cow's milk and is perfect for this dish. Other blue-veined cheeses, like the French Roquefort, are made from sheep's milk and have a slightly more pronounced flavor.

1 Preheat the oven to 375°. Arrange the walnuts in a single layer on a sheet pan lined with a Silpat, parchment paper, or aluminum foil and bake until fragrant, about 7 minutes. As soon as you can smell them, take them out of the oven and immediately transfer to a dinner plate. (Because of their dense oil content, nuts can go from nicely toasted to burnt very quickly and will continue to cook even after they are out of the oven.) Set aside.

2 In a large saucepan, bring the water and salt to a boil over medium-high heat.

3 Add the grits in a slow, steady stream, stirring them into the liquid as you do so with either a wire whisk or a wooden spoon. Lower the heat to medium-low or low and whisk or stir constantly for 2 minutes (this will prevent lumps). Continue to cook, uncovered, stirring every few minutes with a spoon. The grits should be moving, with a few little bubbles breaking at the surface, but not quite simmering. Cook until grits are thick, soft, and creamy, about 35 minutes.

4 Remove from the heat and stir in the cream, followed immediately by the cheese. Stir until the cheese melts and the grits are fragrant. Serve at once with toasted walnuts scattered across each portion.

15

Classic Pimento Cheese

CONTEMPORARY **KRYPTONITE PIMENTO CHEESE**

INTERNATIONAL **SWISS TARTINE**

When I was a food writer at the *Augusta Chronicle* in Georgia, I interviewed a woman who described pimento cheese as "a spoonful of summer." More than just a snack or sandwich filling, pimento cheese is a deeply meaningful food for most southerners. Augusta is home to one of golf's most celebrated tournaments, the Masters. The Augusta National golf course is, among other things, famous for the thousands of pimento cheese sandwiches, wrapped in green waxed paper, that it sells during that tournament.

I love pimento cheese so much, but I used to make it only on special occasions because I was prone to eating it for breakfast, lunch, and dinner (and a few snacks in between). Then I developed this healthier version, which I call Kryptonite Pimento Cheese, and hallelujah, pimento cheese was back in my life on a regular basis. Hint: Both versions are superb served with Wheat Thins crackers.

Swiss Tartine is fabulous because it can be made ahead and just smeared on an open-faced baguette and toasted. Its flavors will take you straight to the Swiss Alps.

Classic Pimento Cheese

*Makes 3½ cups—
plenty for 18 people
as an appetizer*

My eldest daughter's preschool teacher, Miss Martha, has lived in Augusta her entire life. I was new to the area and had yet to make many friends, so Martha took me under her wing. She taught me her secret to making the best pimento cheese. "There's a synergy between these few simple ingredients," I can still hear her saying in her velvety-rich Augusta accent as she stirred together shredded cheese, chopped pimento, a little onion, and mayo. It's simply magical.

- 2 cups shredded sharp cheddar cheese
- 2 cups mild cheddar cheese
- 2 teaspoons grated onion*
- ½ cup chopped pimento (roasted red pepper), drained
- 2 tablespoons juice from the pimentos
- 1 cup real mayonnaise (preferably the South's favorite, Duke's, if you can get it)
- 2 dashes cayenne pepper, or more to taste

1 Combine the shredded cheeses in a mixing bowl and add the onion, pimento, pimento juice, mayo, and cayenne. Mix well with a spoon or rubber spatula. Store, covered, in the refrigerator for up to 3 days. Serve with crackers or as a filling for sandwiches.

*Grate the onion on a box grater or, better yet, a Microplane—it should be almost puréed in consistency.

Kryptonite Pimento Cheese

Creamy, tangy pimento cheese is my Kryptonite, my delicious weakness. There are some dishes that simply aren't as good when put through a healthy makeover—but this is not one of them. Through a few modifications and one unorthodox additional ingredient, I've come up with a pimento cheese recipe that can hold its own against the traditional favorite. Don't be thrown by the fish sauce—it doesn't give even a trace of fish flavor; it only adds umami and balances out the sweetness that comes with low-fat mayo. Seriously, hold your nose and use the fish sauce! It's my secret for making *many* dishes more delicious.

Makes 3½ cups—plenty for 18 people as an appetizer

2 cups shredded 2% sharp cheddar cheese
2 cups shredded 2% mild cheddar cheese
3 teaspoons grated onion*
½ cup chopped pimento (roasted red pepper), drained
¼ cup juice from the pimentos
1 teaspoon fish sauce
½ cup low-fat or light mayonnaise (preferably the South's favorite, Duke's, if you can get it)
½ cup plain Greek yogurt
4 dashes cayenne pepper, or more, to taste

1 Combine the shredded cheeses in a mixing bowl and add the onion, pimento, pimento juice, fish sauce, mayo, yogurt, and cayenne. Mix well with a spoon or rubber spatula. Store, covered, in the refrigerator for up to 3 days. Serve with crackers or as a filling for sandwiches.

*Grate the onion on a box grater or, better yet, a Microplane—it should be almost puréed in consistency.

Swiss Tartine

I first saw a tartine, a French open-faced sandwich, when I was fourteen years old and on a school trip in Europe. It was one of those whirlwind bus tours; we saw something like seven cities in ten days. At one point, our bus stopped at a gas station in France for lunch (lunch in a French gas station can be remarkably good). It was there that I spied the most colorful, beautiful open-faced sandwich—a tartine. I bought one that had hard-boiled egg slices and tender asparagus spears on top of a tuna pâté and ate it on the bus. That gas station tartine remains one of my most delicious memories from that trip.

I've pulled inspiration for this recipe from three distinct areas within the Swiss borders: Italian (prosciutto), French (Brie and Dijon), and Alpine (Gruyère). Mix this up, smear it on a nice baguette, and toast until hot and bubbly.

Makes roughly 3 cups (or enough to spread on 2 halves of a large baguette)

8 ounces Brie cheese
1 very small shallot, peeled
3 ounces prosciutto, chopped
2 cups shredded Gruyère cheese
¼ cup sour cream
2 tablespoons dry white wine
2 teaspoons Dijon mustard
Baguette

1 Scrape the Brie from its white skin (it's fine if some of the white skin gets into the mix—it's perfectly edible, just makes the spread a bit lumpy). Discard the skin, and set aside.

2 If you are using a food processor: Place the shallot and prosciutto in the work bowl and pulse for several second intervals for about 30–60 seconds, until both are finely minced. Add the Brie, Gruyère, sour cream, wine, and mustard. Process for 1 minute, scrape down the sides of the bowl, and process again for 30–60 seconds, until almost smooth—it will be slightly bumpy.

3 If you aren't using a food processor: Chop the shallot and prosciutto very fine, and place all of the ingredients in a mixing bowl.
   Mix them with your hands until they are well combined.
4 Preheat the oven to 375°. Spread the cheese mixture over a halved
   baguette or slices of high-quality bread and bake in the oven (or a
   toaster oven set at 375°) until melted and golden. The spread keeps
   for 3–5 days refrigerated or can be spread on bread and frozen for
   up to 3 months.

16

Classic Pinto Beans

CONTEMPORARY **BLACK BEAN STEW WITH SWEET POTATO AND GINGER**

INTERNATIONAL **TUSCAN WHITE BEAN SOUP**

Jack was onto something when he discovered that a few seemingly innocuous beans could grow into a giant stalk: From a cook's perspective, beans are magical! They are the cheapest, most durable of dry goods and also the most versatile, yielding savory, silken soups; complex, winter-warming side dishes; and rich, slow-roasted entrées like French cassoulets.

The health benefits of bean consumption are well documented. Beans are high in antioxidants and soluble fiber. They keep us feeling fuller for longer. Beans are also a wonderful protein source for vegetarians. It's recommended that we eat at least 3 cups of cooked beans each week, and these recipes will give you a head start.

Starting with dried beans will yield the heartiest, most desirable texture, but in case you are short on time, I explain the quick-cook method too. If you are really short on time, using canned beans works—just make sure to rinse canned beans well to get rid of much of the sodium used in the canning process.

Classic Pinto Beans

Makes 8–12 servings

A big pot of pinto beans is a mainstay in many parts of the South, especially in and around the Appalachian Mountains. They are very simple to prepare, super-inexpensive, and a good source of protein and soluble fiber. I use the quick-cooking method to rehydrate dried beans. If you have time to soak the beans overnight, that's even better—just pick up this recipe at step 2. Serve with cornbread for a truly authentic southern dining experience.

1 pound dried pinto beans
1 yellow onion, peeled, cut in half
1 smoked ham hock, 1 smoked turkey wing,
    or 4 ounces raw bacon (not chopped)
½ teaspoon cayenne pepper
4 teaspoons kosher or sea salt

In case you need to use canned beans: 1 pound of dried beans that have been soaked and cooked is the equivalent of three or four 15-ounce cans.

1 Pick through the dried beans and remove any broken beans or small pebbles (beans are mechanically harvested and sometimes carry along debris). Place the beans in an 8-quart (or very large) pot and cover with water by 3 inches. Cover the pot and bring the liquid to a boil over medium-high heat. Uncover the pot, stir, and continue to boil for 2 minutes. Cover the pot and turn off the heat. Allow the beans to sit in the hot liquid undisturbed for 1 hour.

2 Drain the beans in a colander, then rinse and drain again. Rinse out the cooking pot. Pour the beans back into the pot and fill with enough water to cover the beans by 2 inches. Add the onions; the ham hock, turkey wing, or bacon; and the cayenne. Don't add the salt at this point—adding salt to uncooked beans can make them tough.

3 Cover, set over medium heat, and bring to a simmer. Crack the lid and adjust the heat so that the beans simmer gently. Cook for 2 hours. During the last 10 minutes of cooking—once the beans are tender—add the salt, stir, and allow to bubble away for the final 10 minutes. Remove the ham hock, turkey wing, or bacon and the onions and discard. Serve with some of the bean liquor.

Black Bean Stew with Sweet Potato and Ginger

Makes 8–12 servings

Black beans have been deemed a "superfood," and rightly so. Just one cup will fill you up with nutritional goodness and keep you fueled for hours.

This recipe is made even healthier by incorporating sweet potatoes and tomatoes (two other superfoods). The ginger and toasted sesame oil add Asian flavors. Whenever I serve this to a group, it's a hands-down favorite. It makes a gorgeous side dish with grilled chicken, but by switching out the chicken broth for vegetable broth you can turn it into an impressive vegan main course.

1 pound dried black beans
2 tablespoons toasted sesame oil
2-inch piece fresh ginger root, peeled and chopped
    (about 2 heaping tablespoons)
3 fat garlic cloves, minced or pressed
1 large sweet potato, peeled and shredded (about 4 cups)
1 navel orange, stem end trimmed off, the rest
    cut into quarters

½ cup tomato purée or crushed tomatoes

8 cups chicken or vegetable broth

2 teaspoons kosher or sea salt

1 tablespoon sriracha

5 fat (or 7 skinny) green onions, trimmed and thinly sliced

½ cup chopped fresh cilantro

1 Pick through the dried beans and remove any broken beans or small pebbles (beans are mechanically harvested and sometimes carry along debris). Place the beans in an 8-quart (or very large) pot and cover with water by 3 inches. Cover the pot and bring the liquid to a boil over medium-high heat. Uncover the pot, stir, and continue to boil for 2 minutes. Cover the pot and turn off the heat. Allow the beans to sit in the hot liquid undisturbed for 1 hour.

2 Drain the beans in a colander, then rinse and drain them again. Rinse out the cooking pot. Pour the beans back in the pot and fill with enough water to cover the beans by 2 inches. Cover, bring to a simmer, then crack the lid and simmer for 1 hour. Drain and rinse the beans and set aside. Rinse the cooking pot.

3 Pour the sesame oil into the pot and set over medium-high heat. When the oil starts dimpling and is fragrant, add the ginger and garlic, stir well, and cook for 1 minute. Add the beans, sweet potato, orange quarters, tomato purée, and broth. Cover, bring to a strong simmer; uncover, lower the heat to medium-low or low, and simmer gently for 45 minutes. To keep the temperature constant, you can put the lid back on and crack it as needed—you just want to make sure there is a constant, gentle bubble.

4 Remove the orange pieces and discard and add the salt and sriracha. Stir in the green onions and cilantro and serve.

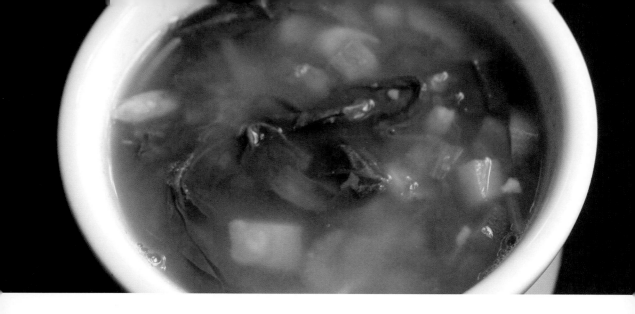

Tuscan White Bean Soup

Mangiafagioli is a common term referring to people from Tuscany, Italy. The term means "bean eaters," and indeed they are. Bean dishes in Tuscany are simply amazing! They are usually simple to prepare, with just a few ingredients, and are always delicious.

Soaking beans overnight will result in the best texture, but the quick-cook method works well too. In case you need to get dinner on the table fast, this recipe explains how to use canned white beans (acceptable in a pinch). Just pick up the recipe in step 3.

12 ounces dried navy or cannellini beans (or 3 [15-ounce] cans cannellini beans, rinsed and drained)

3 medium carrots, peeled

2 medium onions, peeled

4 celery stalks, trimmed

5 garlic cloves, peeled

2 large red-skinned potatoes

12 cups chicken broth (or vegetable broth to make this vegetarian)

2 zucchini, trimmed and cut into ½-inch pieces

3 cups baby spinach, well washed

2 medium tomatoes, chopped

½ teaspoon red pepper flakes
1½ tablespoons fresh thyme leaves
½ tablespoon roughly chopped fresh rosemary leaves
Kosher or sea salt, to taste
Parmesan cheese, to taste

1 Pick through the dried beans and remove any broken beans or small pebbles (beans are mechanically harvested and sometimes carry along debris). Place the beans in an 8-quart (or very large) pot and cover with water by 3 inches. Toss in 1 of the carrots, 1 of the onions, and 2 of the celery stalks. Cover the pot and bring the liquid to a boil over medium-high heat. Uncover the pot, stir, and continue to boil for 2 minutes. Cover the pot and turn off the heat. Allow the beans to sit in the hot liquid undisturbed for 1 hour.

2 Drain the beans in a colander. Remove and discard the carrot, celery, and onion, then rinse and drain the beans again. Rinse out the cooking pot. Pour the beans back into the pot and fill with enough water to cover the beans by 2 inches. Cover, bring to a simmer, then crack the lid and simmer for 1 hour. Drain and rinse the beans and return them to the cooking pot.

3 Chop the remaining carrots, onion, and celery stalks into small pieces, mince or press the garlic, and cut the potato into 1-inch cubes. Add the vegetables to the beans.

4 Add the chicken broth. Cover and bring to a gentle simmer, then uncover and simmer for 1 hour (or, if using canned beans, simmer just 15 minutes), then mash slightly with a potato masher or with an immersion blender—just enough to leave half of the vegetables whole and the soup chunky.

5 Add the zucchini, spinach, tomatoes, red pepper flakes, thyme, and rosemary. Cover the pot and bring the soup to a simmer. Remove the cover and simmer gently for 20 minutes. Taste and season with salt, if desired.

6 Ladle the soup into bowls and sprinkle with the Parmesan cheese. This keeps for up to three days in the refrigerator (the flavor is even better on day three).

Classic Sweet Potato Casserole

CONTEMPORARY **CRISPY SWEET POTATO OVEN FRIES**

INTERNATIONAL **WEST AFRICAN SWEET POTATO AND PEANUT SOUP**

Sweet potatoes are indigenous not only to North, Central, and South America but also to Africa and Asia. They are powerfully nutritious: One medium sweet potato will supply 300 percent of the vitamin A you need for the day. Sweet potatoes are also a good source of fiber and are high in manganese, copper, pantothenic acid (vitamin B5), and vitamin B6. Cooking and eating the skin is even better for you.

As with white potatoes, there are countless ways to prepare sweet potatoes. Simmering, steaming, frying, roasting, baking, grilling, even microwaving sweet potatoes will transform the starchy, dense root vegetable into a supple, slightly sweet base to which myriad flavors and seasonings can be applied.

The classic casserole puts the sweet in sweet potato and is a marvelous complement to savory dishes like holiday roasts. The crispy oven fries recipe uses a secret method of precooking that allows the fries to retain their soft interior while still cooking up satisfyingly crunchy. And if you've never had African sweet potato and peanut soup, this is the one to try. It's to die for!

Classic Sweet Potato Casserole

"Oh, my mama makes the best topping for her sweet potato casserole," my friend Monica told me. Monica was raised in Knoxville, Tennessee, and although she's lived in North Carolina for nearly twenty years, she still considers Knoxville home. Monica's speech, her entire bearing, slows down considerably when she talks about the food she grew up eating: "We're not marshmallow people. Mama puts a crunchy pecan and brown sugar topping on her sweet potato casserole. It's the best . . ."—and she trails off, deep in memories of Thanksgivings past.

Thus began my quest to make a classic sweet potato casserole to rival the one my southern friend grew up eating. When I finally felt I had achieved that, I marched my sweet potato casserole down the street to Monica's house and stood in front of her as she tried it. "Oh my God," Monica said softly. The inflection and tone of her voice reminded me of someone holding an adorable puppy for the first time—pure love tinged with mystery, as in, "How this could be?" "Jenny, this is it. This is just like my mama's!"

FOR THE CASSEROLE
½ cup milk
2 eggs, whisked
1 teaspoon vanilla
Dash of nutmeg
3 cups mashed sweet potatoes (3 medium
   sweet potatoes, microwaved)
¾ cup granulated sugar
4 tablespoons melted butter
¼ teaspoon kosher or sea salt

FOR THE STREUSEL
¼ teaspoon kosher or sea salt
¾ cup lightly packed light brown sugar
1 cup pecan pieces (chopped pecans)
½ cup all-purpose flour
6 tablespoons cold butter, cubed

HOW TO MICROWAVE A SWEET POTATO

Pierce the skin of the sweet potato all over, about 6 times, with a sharp knife or a fork. Place on a microwavable plate and microwave at full power for 5–8 minutes (the time will vary from oven to oven and based on the size of the sweet potato). The potato is cooked when the skin is crisp and the flesh inside is completely tender.

1. For the casserole: Preheat the oven to 350°. Butter a 9 × 11-inch or 3-quart baking dish.

2. In a medium bowl, whisk the milk, eggs, vanilla, and nutmeg together and set aside. In a separate mixing bowl, stir together the sweet potatoes, granulated sugar, butter, and salt. Add the milk mixture and stir until completely incorporated. Pour into the prepared baking dish and make the streusel.

3. In a small bowl, mix the salt, brown sugar, pecans, and flour together. Using a fork or your fingers, "cut in" the butter—that is, distribute it evenly in the flour, until the mixture looks like coarse crumbs. Take care not to work it so far that the butter softens and the streusel turns pastelike. Scatter the streusel evenly over the top of the casserole and bake for 45–60 minutes, or until the streusel is golden.

Crispy Sweet Potato Oven Fries

Makes 4–6 servings

These oven fries are crisp, sweet, slightly spicy, and salty—in other words, addictive. This is a foolproof way of making crispy oven-baked sweet potato fries. There are a few tricks to it, but there's nothing complicated or difficult. Just give yourself, and your sweet potatoes, time to follow the steps.

> 2 pounds sweet potatoes (about 2 large)
> 2 tablespoons cornstarch
> ⅓ cup plus 1 tablespoon freshly grated Parmesan cheese
> ¼ teaspoon cayenne pepper (optional)
> 2 tablespoons peanut oil or melted coconut oil
> Popcorn salt, to taste

1 Peel the sweet potatoes. Cut ½ inch off of the end tips of each potato. Cut a thin slice off of one side of the potato lengthwise, then turn the potato to rest on that side (this will hold the otherwise roly-poly potato steady). Now slice the potatoes into ½-inch-thick slices, and then cut each slice into ½-inch-wide sticks. Place the sweet potato sticks in a large bowl of cool water as you go. Soak the potato sticks for at least 1 hour, up to 24 hours.

Soaking the sliced sweet potatoes in water for at least an hour makes them crispy; soaking them removes much of their starch. Coating with cornstarch will also help in crisping.

Popcorn salt is very fine, much finer than table salt, and makes a great finishing salt for these sweet potato fries (or any other fries) because it sticks to them really well.

2   Preheat the oven to 425°. Pull the sweet potatoes out of the cloudy soaking water and rinse under cool water. Dab dry with paper towels. Working in batches, place the sweet potato sticks in a single layer on a microwave-safe plate. Microwave at full power for 2 minutes, then flip them over and cook 2 minutes longer. Continue with the rest of the sticks until all are semi-cooked and pliable. Dry them all very well with paper towels.

3   Combine the cornstarch, Parmesan, and cayenne, if using, in a small bowl and set aside. Place half of the cooked potato sticks into a gallon-size zip-top bag and drizzle in 1 tablespoon of the oil. Carefully toss the bag around so that all of the sticks get lightly coated. Now toss in half of the cornstarch/Parmesan mixture, zip up the top, and toss again so that all sticks are lightly coated.

4   Spray a large sheet pan with nonstick cooking spray and arrange the sweet potato sticks in a single layer, not letting them touch each other—don't crowd the pan. Bake for 15 minutes; they will soften a bit and begin to turn a deeper orange. Remove the sticks from the oven and flip them over, then bake for 15 minutes longer, or until they are a golden brown (dark brown in spots) and crispy. Remove from the oven and immediately season with the popcorn salt. Allow to cool for 5 minutes; while you wait, they will crisp up even more.

West African Sweet Potato and Peanut Soup

Makes 8 servings

This soup changed my life. That may sound overly dramatic, but I am serious: One slurp of this soup forever shifted the way I thought about groundnuts. Its silky, savory, spicy flavor is unexpected and addictive.

I first tasted a version of peanut soup when I was six years old and on our annual family vacation in Colonial Williamsburg in Virginia. That first cup of peanut soup is one of my fondest food memories. I am not a peanut butter and jelly fan, so it opened my eyes to the fact that peanuts weren't solely meant to be paired with sweet jelly or honey.

Peanuts and their farming and cooking methods came to this country with West African slaves, which is why peanut soup became a dish of the South. Although soup recipes vary from country to country and region to region, the groundnut soups found in West African countries have commonalities. In addition to peanuts and chicken broth, they often have sweet potatoes and tomatoes and are delightfully spicy.

This recipe is remarkably simple (put everything in the pot, simmer, and purée), yet it's restaurant quality. I only make it a few times a year, though; its delicately sweet and boldly spicy flavor is so good that I inevitably eat the entire pot myself before anyone else in the family has a fighting chance.

2 sweet potatoes, peeled and cut into 1-inch cubes

1 large yellow onion, peeled and roughly chopped

2 celery stalks, trimmed and roughly chopped

2 tablespoons tomato paste

½–1 teaspoon red pepper flakes or 1–2 tablespoons sambal oelek

8 cups chicken broth

1 cup natural (unsweetened) peanut butter

1 teaspoon kosher or sea salt

1 lime cut into wedges

1 Pile the sweet potatoes, onion, celery, tomato paste, and red pepper flakes into a 3-quart soup pot, then add the chicken broth. Turn the heat to high and bring the soup just to a boil, then immediately reduce the heat to medium-low and simmer, uncovered, for 15 minutes, or until the sweet potatoes are very tender and easily squished with the back of a spoon or fork.

2 Use an immersion blender to purée the soup (or transfer the soup to a stand blender and purée). Once smooth, add the peanut butter and salt and whisk until well incorporated. Heat through and serve with limes wedges to squeeze into the soup just before eating.

18

Classic Deviled Eggs

CONTEMPORARY **HERBY OLIVE OIL DEVILED EGGS**

INTERNATIONAL **TRUFFLED DEVILS**

A deviled egg feels sort of luxurious to me. When I was growing up, my mother had a strict rule against snacking, especially near mealtimes. So the fact that on some occasions deviled eggs were offered *before* a meal—this was a cause for celebration! The combination of cold, firm egg white cradling a richly seasoned, creamy yolk makes it an old-school favorite.

Deviled eggs aren't exclusive to the South, but they sure are beloved here. I'd always had a hard time removing the egg shell without causing pock marks on the cooked egg white until my cousin Steve shared his secret: steaming the eggs rather than simmering them. I use my cousin's method every time I make deviled eggs now, and it truly works! No more pockmarks—just smooth, glistening hard-boiled eggs. Also, using fresh eggs is actually a no-no when making deviled eggs. Older eggs (held about 7 days in the refrigerator) will yield easier-peeling shells, but not to worry—steaming even works on fresh eggs.

Classic deviled eggs, whipped up with sweet pickle relish, taste almost refreshing with their sweet and tangy filling. The herby olive oil eggs are my father's favorite because of their own lightness and fresh, herbaceous notes. But it's the truffled devils that are my undoing. I am powerless in the face of their umami-bomb flavor.

opposite: Classic Deviled Eggs

Classic Deviled Eggs

Makes 12 deviled eggs

The sweet pickle relish plays nicely off the rich egg yolks—it also adds a little crunch. This is a great go-to recipe that is easy to put together—perfect for picnics or family gatherings or on a buffet table. I like deviled eggs to have a firm, slightly stiff yolk mixture. If you prefer gooier stuffed eggs, use more mayonnaise—start by adding 1 teaspoon at a time.

6 hard-boiled eggs
1½ teaspoons Dijon mustard
1½ tablespoons sweet pickle relish
2 tablespoons mayonnaise
¼ teaspoon kosher or sea salt

1 Using a sharp knife, slice the eggs in half lengthwise. (Don't use a serrated knife since it will leave marks on the egg white.) Pop the yolks into a small bowl and either mash them with a fork or push them through a small sieve (the latter will yield a smoother filling). Add the mustard, relish, mayo, and salt and stir well to combine.

2 Scoop the filling into a plastic sandwich bag. Some people say not to fill the eggs until just before serving because the filled eggs sometimes "weep" or look as if they are sweating, but I've not had that issue with this recipe. Fill right away or wait—it's up to you. If you decide to wait, stash the filling and egg whites in the refrigerator until ready to fill.

3 When you are ready to fill the eggs, line the egg whites up on a serving platter. Snip off the corner of the sandwich bag, so that there is a ½-inch opening, then gently squeeze the filling into the egg whites.

HOW TO MAKE PERFECT HARD-BOILED EGGS

1 Put a steamer insert* in a pot and add enough water to come up 1 inch below the steamer (you don't want water bubbling into the steamer or touching the eggs). Cover, either with a tight-fitting lid or with foil, and place over high heat. Once the water is boiling, carefully place the eggs in the steamer, replace the cover, and steam for exactly 12 minutes.

2 Meanwhile, make an ice bath—that is, fill a large bowl with ice and cold water.

3 When the eggs have finished cooking, immediately transfer them to the ice bath. Allow them to sit for 10 minutes.

4 Remove the eggs and gently crack the shells on the counter's surface (not its edge, as that may push some of the shell into the cooked white), then peel the eggs under cold running water. Set them aside until ready to create your deviled eggs!

*If you don't have a pot with a steamer insert, you can use a metal colander or wire rack that fits in any pot. As with the steamer insert, pour water into the pot until it's 1 inch below the colander or rack.

Herby Olive Oil Deviled Eggs

Makes 12 deviled eggs

By swapping out mayo for olive oil and plain yogurt in this recipe, I replace refined fats with heart-healthy fats. These are eggs most anyone can indulge in. If you love the flavor of high-quality extra-virgin olive oil, you will love these; if you are not so fond of that flavor, you can use a light olive oil and still reap the health benefits.

6 hard-boiled eggs
1½ tablespoons extra-virgin olive oil (this is where
    to splurge on the expensive stuff)
1½ tablespoons plain Greek yogurt
1 teaspoon lemon juice
¼ teaspoon kosher or sea salt
1 tablespoon chopped fresh tarragon
    (or dill, chervil, or basil)
1 tablespoon chopped fresh parsley
1½ tablespoons chopped fresh chives

1 Using a sharp knife, slice the eggs in half lengthwise. (Don't use a serrated knife since it will leave marks on the egg white.) Pop the yolks into a small bowl and either mash them with a fork or push them through a small sieve (the latter will yield a smoother filling). Add the olive oil, yogurt, lemon juice, salt, and herbs and stir well to combine.

2 Scoop the filling into a plastic sandwich bag. Some people say not to fill the eggs until just before serving because the filled eggs sometimes "weep" or look as if they are sweating, but I've not had that issue with this recipe. Fill now or wait—it's up to you. If you decide to wait, stash the filling and egg whites in the refrigerator until ready to fill.

3 When you are ready to fill the eggs, line the egg whites up on a serving platter. Snip off the corner of the sandwich bag, so that there is a ½-inch opening, then gently squeeze the filling into the egg whites.

Herby Olive Oil Deviled Eggs

Truffled Devils

Makes 12 deviled eggs

These became my favorite style of deviled eggs the moment I made them. Packed with savory umami notes from truffle oil, truffle salt, and Parmesan, these devilishly delicious eggs also have a pleasing crunch that plays off the soft yolk beautifully. Warm, crunchy, and savory, they make a wonderful dinner served with a green salad.

> 6 hard-boiled eggs
> 2 tablespoons mayonnaise
> 1 teaspoon truffle oil
> ¼ teaspoon truffle salt
> 2 tablespoons butter
> ¼ cup panko bread crumbs
> ¼ cup freshly grated Parmesan cheese

1 Using a sharp knife, slice the eggs in half lengthwise. (Don't use a serrated knife since it will leave marks on the egg white.) Pop the yolks into a small bowl and either mash them with a fork or push them through a small sieve (the latter will yield a smoother filling). Add the mayonnaise, truffle oil, and truffle salt and stir well to combine.

2 Using a small spoon, fill the egg halves with the yoke mixture. Wipe off the spoon, wet it under cool water, and use the back of it to smooth the tops of the filled eggs so that they are somewhat flat—they don't have to be perfect. At this point you can either keep the eggs in the refrigerator for up to a day, until you're ready to sauté them, or carry on with the recipe.

3 Heat a sauté pan over medium heat, spray it with nonstick cooking spray, and add 1 tablespoon of the butter. While you are waiting for the butter to froth, pour the bread crumbs and the Parmesan into a saucer or small plate, gently stir them together, and dip the eggs in, filled side down. When the butter has frothed and the frothing has subsided, put half of the eggs in the pan, filling/crumb side down, and cook gently for 3 minutes. To remove the eggs, slide a thin spatula with one quick motion underneath each egg (so as to keep the Parmesan crust intact) and remove it to a serving dish. Add the remaining butter to the pan and repeat the process with the remaining eggs. Serve immediately.

19.

Classic Skillet Cornbread

CONTEMPORARY **SKINNY CORNBREAD**

INTERNATIONAL **SOPA PARAGUAYA**

The buttery scent of cornbread baking in the oven sends my children into a state of salivating anxiety. Not dissimilar to rabid dogs, my four daughters pace back and forth across the kitchen floor waiting for the hot, crispy, crunchy bread to emerge from the oven in its jet-black, well-worn, and well-loved cast-iron skillet.

As beloved as cornbread is in the South—or maybe precisely for that reason—it can be an acrimonious subject to discuss with southern cooks. First of all, there's the sugar debate: Should you add sugar, or leave it out? Southern cornbread is not supposed to be sweet, as cornbread tends to be in other parts of the country, and some cooks are adamant about forgoing sugar. My recipe calls for a little sugar. In the same way that salt elevates savory dishes, a little sugar here brings out the natural sweetness of the cornmeal—but this is far from a sweet cornbread.

Second, southern cornbread is dryer and less cakelike than non-southern cornbread, because there is very little flour in it. (You'll find some recipes that don't call for any flour at all.)

Third, southern cornbread is often baked in a cast-iron skillet. This really does make a difference in the final product, giving the cornbread that crispy brown bottom and sides that people love. A cast-iron skillet is a useful pan to have for many other uses as well—it's well worth buying one.

Southern cornbread has a crunchy, dry crumb that is the perfect accompaniment for a steaming bowl of pinto beans or stew, and it fits perfectly on a dinner buffet table. Amazingly, the skinny cornbread recipe lacks nothing—it's slightly sweet and thoroughly satisfying. Sopa Paraguaya is something altogether different, spongy, cheesy, and satiating—not your typical cornbread, but not to be missed, either.

Classic Skillet Cornbread

Makes 8 servings

As the name suggests, you will need a cast-iron skillet for this recipe. You will find that the cast-iron skillet is a useful kitchen item; I use mine whenever I sauté or fry. If you don't want to spend the money on a new one, look at secondhand stores—I have found several cast-iron skillets in thrift shops. And don't be put off by a little rust: Simply buff it off with a steel wool pad and follow the seasoning steps on page 166.

> 5 tablespoons butter, divided
> 1½ cups medium- or fine-ground cornmeal
> ½ cup all-purpose flour
> 1 tablespoon granulated sugar
> 1 teaspoon kosher or sea salt
> 1 tablespoon baking powder
> 1 cup buttermilk
> 2 eggs, whisked

1 Place a 10-inch cast-iron skillet in the oven and preheat the oven to 400°. Melt 4 tablespoons of the butter. In a large bowl, combine the cornmeal, flour, granulated sugar, salt, and baking powder. Add the buttermilk and eggs and stir to blend, then add the melted butter and mix again; it shouldn't have any lumps but will look grainy from the cornmeal.

2 Use oven mitts to remove the skillet from the oven and put the remaining butter in it to melt. Roll the skillet around so that the butter coats the bottom and sides, then quickly pour in the cornmeal batter. Bake for 20 minutes, or until the sides are golden and the middle is firm. Allow to cool for at least 10 minutes before slicing.

Skinny Cornbread

This cornbread is so flavorful and so moist, yet it contains no butter or shortening (puréed fresh or frozen corn kernels in the batter is the secret). This is one of my go-to recipes because it's also a snap to make.

Makes 8 servings

1½ cups finely ground cornmeal
½ cup white whole-wheat flour
1 teaspoon kosher or sea salt
1 tablespoon baking powder
1 cup fresh or frozen corn kernels (thawed)
1 cup buttermilk
1 tablespoon honey or agave nectar
3 tablespoons melted coconut oil
2 large eggs, whisked

1 Preheat the oven to 400°. Spray a 9 × 11-inch baking dish with nonstick cooking spray and set aside. In a large bowl, combine the cornmeal, flour, salt, and baking powder and set aside.

2 Using an immersion blender or traditional blender, purée the corn kernels, buttermilk, honey or agave, and coconut oil together until smooth, about 30 seconds. Add the eggs and blend for about 5 seconds, just to evenly combine the eggs with the wet ingredients.

3 Add the wet ingredients to the dry ingredients and stir until well combined and uniform, scraping down the sides of the bowl. Pour the batter into the prepared baking dish and bake for 20 minutes. Allow it to rest for at least 10 minutes before cutting.

AN EASY WAY TO SEASON, CLEAN, AND MAINTAIN YOUR NEW CAST-IRON SKILLET

Wash: Scrub your new skillet with soapy water and the scrubber side of a sponge.

Season: Dry completely and place it on the stovetop over high heat for about 2–3 minutes, until it's smoking hot. Use a paper towel to rub a very small amount (½–1 teaspoon) of vegetable oil or lard into the hot pan, turn off the heat, and allow the pan to cool completely. Repeat this seasoning process two more times. Now your skillet is seasoned.

Clean up: After using your skillet, wash with warm, soapy water and the scrubber side of a sponge (using soap in a seasoned skillet is a sacrilege to most southern cooks, but stay with me). Dry immediately and thoroughly, then place on the stovetop over high heat for 2–3 minutes, until smoking hot. Use a paper towel to rub ½–1 teaspoon vegetable oil into the hot skillet. Keep it over high heat until it just starts to smoke, then remove it from the heat and allow it to cool completely (you don't need to repeat this process) before putting it away.

Sopa Paraguaya

This cheesy dish is half cornbread, half soufflé, and 100 percent delicious. Its name means "Paraguayan soup." There are numerous stories about why a bread dish is called a soup, but alas, none that I found can be confirmed. For me at least, it's more about the flavor than about the origin of the name. Sopa Paraguaya can be found in Paraguay, northeastern Argentina, and other South American regions. It's very moist, cheesy, and spongy. The method of whisking the egg whites into stiff peaks, then incorporating them, is similar to preparing soufflé, except you don't have to worry about this one "falling" once it's pulled from the oven—it doesn't rise like a delicate soufflé to begin with, but it does capture some of a soufflé's lightness.

Makes 12 servings

4 tablespoons butter (plus more for the baking dish)
1 large yellow onion, peeled and chopped (2 cups)
1 pound fresh or frozen corn kernels (thawed)
2 cups cornmeal
1 teaspoon kosher or sea salt
1 tablespoon baking powder

2 cups milk
4 eggs, yolks and whites separated
1 cup cottage cheese
1 cup shredded mozzarella cheese
½ teaspoon cream of tartar

1 Preheat the oven to 375°. Butter (or spray with nonstick cooking spray) a 9 × 11-inch or 3-quart baking dish. Melt the butter in a sauté pan over medium heat and add the onions. Sauté, stirring every few minutes, until the onions are soft and translucent. Add the corn and continue cooking for just a minute or two, then remove from the heat so that the mixture cools slightly.

2 Mix the cornmeal, salt, and baking powder together in a large mixing bowl. In a separate bowl, whisk the milk and egg yolks together and stir this into the cornmeal mixture until fully incorporated. Add the onions and corn and stir well to combine. Add both the cheeses and mix until well combined.

3 Using a hand mixer or a wire whisk beat the egg whites with the cream of tartar until stiff peaks form (see the tips on how to whip egg whites into stiff peaks). Very gently, fold the egg whites into the cornmeal mixture until well incorporated. Pour the batter into the prepared baking dish and bake for 30 minutes. Allow to cool for at least 20 minutes before slicing. It will be very heavy and moist and, best of all, cheesy.

HOW TO "FOLD"

Place a third of the whipped egg whites into the center of the cornmeal mixture. Use a rubber spatula or wooden spoon to gently cut down into the center of the cornmeal mixture, move the spatula or spoon along the bottom of the bowl, then come up the other side, bringing some of the cornmeal mixture from the bottom to the top and moving some of the egg white from the top to the bottom. Rotate the bowl and repeat, incorporating a third of the whipped egg whites at a time. Be careful not to overmix—that will make the whipped egg whites lose their volume.

A FOOLPROOF WAY TO WHIP EGG WHITES INTO STIFF PEAKS

1 If you can plan ahead, leave the eggs out at room temperature for 30 minutes before whipping—they will whip faster and be more stable.
2 Use a copper, stainless steel, or glass bowl—never plastic.
3 Make sure that the bowl and beaters or whisk are completely clean, free of fat (like oil, grease, or egg yolk) or water. The egg whites will first become frothy, then soft, and finally stiff. Add the cream of tartar once the eggs are frothy. It's important not to overbeat the whites; you'll know they are overbeaten if they look dry. Also, use them as soon as they are beaten, because if they sit too long they will deflate and possibly separate.

20

Classic Buttermilk Biscuits

CONTEMPORARY VEGAN BISCUITS

INTERNATIONAL BRITISH BUTTERMILK SCONES

Making biscuits from scratch can seem daunting to many home cooks, but there's nothing to fear. I'll give you a few tricks to making biscuits that are light, tender, and fluffy; follow these steps and you will have success.

There's really no wrong way to eat a classic buttermilk biscuit. They are wonderful stuffed with pimento cheese or slices of country ham, smeared with butter, drizzled with honey, or eaten hot, straight out of the oven. The idea of vegan biscuits may seem counterintuitive, but trust me, they are fantastic and not just for vegetarians. Scones are deservedly popular because they can act as a carrier for so many flavors—sweet, dried fruits, hunks of white chocolate, or maybe a bacon/sharp cheddar combo.

Classic Buttermilk Biscuits

Makes 12 biscuits

Well-made buttermilk biscuits are unforgettable, and are actually easy to make. If you are making them for a special meal, try to time it so that they come out just as you want to serve them—they are exquisite warm from the oven.

I've always made biscuits using butter, but many southerners prefer using lard or shortening—it's just a matter of preference. However, do use the specific flour called for in each recipe. I know that sounds bossy, but there is a reason: Different types of flours (whole-wheat, white whole-wheat, winter wheat, or all-purpose) will react differently to liquids. These recipes were developed using the specific flours listed. Follow the recipes exactly, and you'll have success!

2 cups soft winter wheat flour (like White Lily brand), chilled in freezer for at least 30 minutes, plus ¼ cup for kneading and rolling

½ teaspoon baking soda

2 teaspoons baking powder

1 teaspoon kosher or sea salt

6 tablespoons very cold butter (in one piece, not cut up)

1 cup very cold buttermilk

SOME BISCUIT-MAKING TIPS

1 When making biscuits, make sure the three main ingredients (butter, buttermilk, and even flour) are ice cold—keep the butter and buttermilk in the refrigerator and the flour in the freezer (don't worry, it won't freeze).

2 Make sure the oven has time to preheat properly (up to 20 minutes).

3 Don't overwork the dough: That will make the biscuits tough. I'll guide you in the directions.

4 Cutting the biscuits in squares practically eliminates the need to reroll the dough, as you would if using a round biscuit cutter. Rerolling the dough overworks it and can result in tough biscuits.

1 Preheat the oven to 425°. Spray a jelly roll pan with nonstick cooking spray or line with parchment paper or a Silpat.

2 Place the flour, baking soda, baking powder, and salt in a large mixing bowl and stir to combine well. Grate the butter directly into the flour using the large holes of a box grater. Using a fork or pastry blender, "cut in" the butter—that is, distribute it evenly in the flour, until the mixture looks like coarse crumbs. Work quickly: You want everything to remain as cold as possible. Add the buttermilk all at once and stir with a rubber spatula, just until the mixture begins to become a shaggy dough. Flour your hands with 1 tablespoon of the flour, and fold the dough over onto itself, repeating 6–8 times, until you can form a ball (it won't be as smooth as bread or pizza dough).

3 Sprinkle 1½ tablespoons of the flour onto a clean work surface and gently flatten the dough ball a bit into the flour, then sprinkle the remaining flour on top of the dough. Roll out the dough very gently with a rolling pin, shaping it into a square or rectangle, until it's ¾–1 inch thick. Trim the edges straight with a large, sharp knife, then cut the dough into 12 squares (4 rows of 3). Place the squares on the prepared pan so that they are touching each other (this will help them bake up tall). Bake for 12–17 minutes, or until the tops are golden. Best served immediately.

Classic Buttermilk Biscuits

Vegan Biscuits

Makes 12 biscuits

Vegan biscuits seem to defy the very idea of biscuits, since buttermilk and butter are two of the main ingredients in the classic recipe. But these vegan versions really are delicious. It's actually not a far stretch to go from Classic Buttermilk Biscuits to Vegan, by using vegan "butter" and almond "milk." Adding white whole-wheat flour adds another layer of healthy ingredients to this recipe.

1 cup white whole-wheat flour (I like King Arthur brand for this) or plain whole-wheat flour, chilled in the freezer for at least 30 minutes

1 cup soft winter wheat flour (like White Lily brand), chilled in the freezer for at least 30 minutes, plus ¼ cup for kneading and rolling

½ teaspoon baking soda

2 teaspoons baking powder

1 teaspoon kosher or sea salt

6 tablespoons vegan butter (in one piece, not cut up), chilled in the freezer for 10–20 minutes

1 cup plain almond milk

1. Preheat the oven to 425°. Spray a jelly roll pan with nonstick cooking spray or line with parchment paper or a Silpat.

2. Place both of the flours, the baking soda, the baking powder, and the salt in a large mixing bowl and stir to combine well. Grate the vegan butter directly into the flour using the large holes of a box grater. Using a fork or pastry blender, "cut in" the butter—that is, distribute it evenly in the flour, until the mixture looks like coarse crumbs. Work quickly: You want everything to remain as cold as possible. Add the almond milk all at once and stir with a rubber spatula just until the mixture begins to become a shaggy dough. Flour your hands with 1 tablespoon of the winter wheat flour and fold the dough over onto itself, repeating 6–8 times, until you can form a ball (it won't be as smooth as bread or pizza dough).

3. Sprinkle 1½ tablespoons of the winter wheat flour onto a clean work surface and gently flatten the dough ball a bit into the flour, then sprinkle the remaining flour on top of the dough. Roll out the dough very gently with a rolling pin, shaping it into a square or rectangle, until it's ¾–1 inch thick. Trim the edges straight with a large, sharp knife, then cut the dough into 12 squares (4 rows of 3). Place the squares on the prepared pan so that they are touching each other (this will help them bake up tall). Bake for 12–17 minutes, or until the tops are golden. Best served immediately.

British Buttermilk Scones

Makes 12–14 scones

I grew up drinking iced tea but learned to relish, even crave, hot tea soon after our family moved to a picturesque old farm in chilly north-western England. We lived in a 250-year-old converted brick barn that was quiet and drafty. We moved there in July, and I remember phoning my husband at work a few days later to ask him how to turn on the heat in the house.

"Having a cuppa" (drinking hot tea) is literally a way of life in that Beatrix Potter part of the world. It's unheard-of for someone (whether friend, neighbor, or repairman) not to be offered a cup of tea when at your home.

The perfect accompaniment to tea is a scone. Slathering the scone in clotted cream and jam makes it into an event called a "cream tea." I love that drinking a hot beverage and eating a baked good can be so easily turned into a small celebration. The garden center in our little village served fabulous cream tea. Gathering on a rainy Saturday there inside the center's warm café with my soggy family, sipping hot tea and munching on scones with clotted cream and raspberry jam, is such a sweet memory from our time there.

2 cups soft winter wheat flour (like White Lily brand),
    chilled in freezer for at least 30 minutes,
    plus ¼ cup for kneading and rolling
½ teaspoon baking soda
2 teaspoons baking powder
1 teaspoon kosher or sea salt
⅓ cup granulated sugar
6 tablespoons very cold butter, in one piece, not cut up
1 large egg
½ cup very cold buttermilk or milk

1 Preheat the oven to 425°. Spray a jelly roll pan with nonstick cooking spray or line with parchment paper or a Silpat.

2 Place the flour, baking soda, baking powder, salt, and sugar in a large mixing bowl and stir to combine well. Grate the butter directly into the flour using the large holes of a box grater. Using a fork or pastry blender, "cut in" the butter—that is, distribute it evenly in the flour, until the mixture looks like coarse crumbs. Work quickly: You want everything to remain as cold as possible.

3 Whisk the egg with the buttermilk or milk and then add it to the dry ingredients all at once; stir with a rubber spatula just until the mixture begins to become a shaggy dough. Flour your hands with 1 tablespoon of the flour and fold the dough over onto itself, repeating 6–8 times, until you can form a ball (it won't be as smooth as bread or pizza dough).

4 Sprinkle 1½ tablespoons of the flour onto a clean work surface and gently flatten the dough ball a bit into the flour, then sprinkle the remaining flour on top of the dough. Roll out the dough very gently with a rolling pin, shaping it into a square or rectangle, until it's ¾ inch thick. Trim the edges straight with a large, sharp knife, cut the dough into 6–7 large squares, then cut each square diagonally, making 12–14 triangles. Place the triangles onto the prepared pan so that they are touching each other (this will help them bake up tall). Bake for 12–17 minutes, until the tops are golden. Best served immediately.

21

Classic Spoon Bread

CONTEMPORARY **SPOON BREAD WITH KALE AND LEMON ZEST**

INTERNATIONAL **JAMBON PERSILLÉ SPOON BREAD**

If you can make grits, you can definitely make spoon bread. Sweet, soft, warm, and buttery, spoon bread makes a fabulous side dish or even a starter, as it's served in some southern restaurants. It's not bread in the traditional sense—it's closer to a soufflé, but don't be intimidated by that. The cooking method for spoon bread is exactly like making grits, only then you add eggs and it becomes airy and light. It's a natural served alongside smoky, salty ham but also pairs well with oven-roasted vegetables (for a vegetarian entrée) or roast chicken.

As in several of the contemporary recipe versions in this book, sometimes making a recipe healthier doesn't necessarily mean taking away ingredients. Adding specific ingredients to a dish, like kale to classic spoon bread, will add nutrition. Adding salty ham, finely chopped parsley, and Camembert to the international version takes this delicate side dish and pushes it to center stage.

opposite: Classic Spoon Bread

Classic Spoon Bread

*Makes 6–8
side-dish servings*

When I was young, probably six or seven years old, my family took a summer vacation to North Carolina's Outer Banks. The rough surf and tall sand dunes were impressive to my little frame, but a memory of equal import was my first encounter with spoon bread.

We drove away from the beach, inland, to a little town where my parents had made reservations at a historic restaurant. This was a big deal because, as I've said, our family didn't eat out often.

The restaurant was in a beautiful old house with worn wooden floorboards, and thick beams holding up the dining room ceiling. I remember that my father ordered soft-shell crabs that oozed pale yellow when he cut into them, my mother ordered flounder that was sautéed tableside with a lemon and caper pan sauce, and I had fried chicken and soft green beans. If I ever eat a meal with you, I may not remember your name, but what you ate will be emblazoned on my memory forever.

After our entrées were served, the waiter came around the table with a casserole dish offering everyone warm spoon bread. I was confused: It wasn't bread, but the server was using a spoon. I gave it a try. It was the most perfectly balanced, genteel dish my tiny taste buds had ever encountered. Slightly sweet, as well as salty, buttery, eggy, soft, and warm. It was so comforting I wanted to take a nap in it.

3 tablespoons butter, divided
2½ cups 2% milk
1 teaspoon kosher or sea salt
1 teaspoon granulated sugar
1 cup finely ground cornmeal
4 eggs, yolks and whites separated
½ teaspoon cream of tartar

1 Preheat the oven to 350°. Grease a 2-quart baking dish with 1 table-spoon of the butter and set aside. Heat the milk, salt, sugar, and remaining butter over medium heat in a 4-quart saucepan, uncovered. Bring just to a simmer; it will go from a simmer to boiling over in a matter of seconds, so watch very closely. As soon as the milk mixture comes to a simmer, slowly pour the cornmeal into the pot in a steady stream, whisking as you go. Turn the heat down to medium-low and continue whisking as the cornmeal thickens, then change to a wooden spoon or heatproof rubber spatula. Stir and cook until the cornmeal pulls away from the bottom and sides of the pan, roughly 4–5 minutes. Remove the pan from the heat and set aside to cool for 10 minutes, stirring occasionally to release more heat.

2 Meanwhile, in a small bowl, beat the egg yolks with a fork until smooth and set aside. Beat the egg whites just until frothy, then add the cream of tartar and beat until stiff peaks form.

3 Mix the egg yolks into the cornmeal and stir until completely combined. Very gently, fold the egg whites into the cornmeal mixture until well incorporated.

4 Pour the mixture into the prepared baking dish and bake for 45 minutes, until puffed and slightly golden. Remove from the oven and slather with butter. Serve immediately.

Classic Spoon Bread

A FOOLPROOF WAY TO WHIP EGG WHITES INTO STIFF PEAKS

1   If you can plan ahead, leave the eggs out at room temperature for 30 minutes before whipping—they will whip faster and be more stable.

2   Use a copper, stainless steel, or glass bowl—never plastic.

3   Make sure that the bowl and beaters or whisk are completely clean, free of fat (like oil, grease, or egg yolk) or water. The egg whites will first become frothy, then soft, and finally stiff. Add the cream of tartar once the eggs are frothy. It's important not to overbeat the whites; you'll know they are overbeaten if they look dry. Also, use them as soon as they are beaten, because if they sit too long they will deflate and possibly separate.

HOW TO "FOLD"

Place a third of the whipped egg whites into the center of the cornmeal mixture. Use a rubber spatula or wooden spoon to gently cut down into the center of the cornmeal mixture, move the spatula or spoon along the bottom of the bowl, then come up the other side, bringing some of the cornmeal mixture from the bottom to the top and moving some of the egg white from the top to the bottom. Rotate the bowl and repeat, incorporating a third of the whipped egg whites at a time. Be careful not to overmix—that will make the whipped egg whites lose their volume.

Spoon Bread with Kale and Lemon Zest

Adding finely shredded fresh kale and the zest of a lemon takes this dish in a fresh and different direction. The lemon zest complements the sweetness of the cornmeal beautifully. Adding kale amps up the nutritional element. If you already love kale, use all four leaves; if not, use just three. In either case, makes sure the leaves are finely chopped.

Makes 6–8
side-dish servings

3 tablespoons butter, divided

3–4 large leaves kale, finely chopped

Zest of 1½ lemons, grated with a Microplane or
    very finely chopped

2½ cups 2% milk

1 teaspoon kosher or sea salt

1 teaspoon granulated sugar

1 cup finely ground cornmeal

4 eggs, yolks and whites separated

½ teaspoon cream of tartar

1 Preheat the oven to 350°. Grease a 2-quart baking dish with 1 table-spoon of the butter and set aside. Fill a 4-quart saucepan three-quarters full of hot water, cover, set it over high heat, and bring the water to a boil. Drop the chopped kale into the boiling water, and as soon as the water begins to boil again, pour it all into a colander and drain the kale well. Set the colander in a bowl (to collect any residual cooking water) and place the lemon zest on top of the hot kale.

2 Wash out the saucepan and add the milk, salt, sugar, and remaining butter. Over medium heat, bring the mixture just to a simmer; it will go from a simmer to boiling over in a matter of seconds, so watch very closely. As soon as it comes to a simmer, slowly pour the cornmeal into the pot in a steady stream, whisking as you go. Turn the heat down to medium-low and continue whisking as the cornmeal thickens, then change to a wooden spoon or heatproof rubber spatula. Stir and cook until the cornmeal pulls away from the bottom and sides of the pan, roughly 4–5 minutes. Remove the pan from the heat and set aside to cool for 10 minutes, stirring occasionally to release more heat. Stir in the kale and lemon zest.

3 Meanwhile, in a small bowl, beat the egg yolks with a fork until smooth and set aside. Beat the egg whites just until frothy, then add the cream of tartar and beat until stiff peaks form.

4 Add the egg yolks to the cornmeal/kale mixture and stir until they are uniformly distributed. Very gently, fold the egg whites into the cornmeal mixture until well incorporated.

5 Pour the mixture into the prepared baking dish and bake for 45 minutes, until puffed and slightly golden. Remove from the oven and slather with butter. Serve immediately.

Jambon Persillé Spoon Bread

During the seven years that our family lived abroad, I only rarely had the treat of taking off with a friend, leaving my husband back at home with our four small children. (Full disclosure: When I would come home from my girls' weekends away, the house was always tidier than when I left.) My favorite travel buddy was my best friend, Dana, and one of our best trips was to the Bourgogne (Burgundy) region. It's in the heart of France and less than 4 hours by car from our homes in Switzerland. We rented a small *gîte* (apartment) in Beaune and marveled at the gorgeous architecture and markets of that historic town, and of course the food.

Dana and I agreed that our favorite food discovery was jambon persillé (parsleyed ham), a sort of terrine in which ham is suspended in gelatin with copious amounts of chopped parsley. I took the best of that recipe (salty ham and lots of freshly chopped parsley) and added Camembert cheese as a nod to France's Normandy region. When you mix ham and Camembert cheese into spoon bread, the result is more than a side dish. Paired with a green salad, it could easily be a main course.

Makes 6–8
side-dish servings

¼ cup roughly chopped shallots

1 cup parsley leaves, well packed

4 ounces high-quality cooked ham

4 ounces Camembert cheese, well chilled

3 tablespoons butter, divided

2½ cups 2% milk

1 teaspoon kosher or sea salt

1 teaspoon granulated sugar

1 cup finely ground cornmeal

4 eggs, yolks and whites separated

1 Place the shallots and parsley in the bowl of a food processor and pulse 5 times (for 1-second intervals), until minced. Add the ham and pulse 5 more times, until everything is finely minced. If you're not using a food processor, just chop everything very fine by hand. Cut the cheese into ½-inch cubes (with or without the white rind). Set it all in the refrigerator.

2 Preheat the oven to 350°. Grease a 2-quart baking dish with 1 tablespoon of the butter and set aside. Heat the milk, salt, sugar, and remaining butter over medium heat in a 4-quart saucepan, uncovered. Bring just to a simmer; it will go from a simmer to boiling over in a matter of seconds, so watch very closely. As soon as it comes to a simmer, slowly pour the cornmeal into the pot in a steady stream, whisking as you go. Turn the heat down to medium-low and continue whisking as the cornmeal thickens,

then change to a wooden spoon or heatproof rubber spatula. Stir and cook until the cornmeal pulls away from the bottom and sides of the pan, roughly 4–5 minutes. Remove the pan from the heat and set aside to cool for 10 minutes, stirring occasionally to release more heat. Stir in the shallots, parsley, ham, and cheese cubes.

3 Meanwhile, in a small bowl, beat the egg yolks with a fork until smooth and set aside. Beat the egg whites just until frothy, then add the cream of tartar and beat until stiff peaks form.

4 Add the egg yolks to the cornmeal mixture and stir until they are uniformly distributed. Very gently, fold the beaten egg whites into the cornmeal mixture.

5 Pour the mixture into the prepared baking dish and bake for 45 minutes, until puffed and slightly golden. Remove from the oven and slather with butter. Serve immediately.

Classic Red Velvet Cake

CONTEMPORARY **BUTTER-FREE RED VELVET CAKE**

INTERNATIONAL **NORWEGIAN SPICED CHOCOLATE CAKE**

Delicate, chocolaty, sweet, spongy—red velvet cake tastes as beautiful as it looks. It used to be that you could only find red velvet in the South and in layer-cake form. Now it's ubiquitous; you can find it across the country in cupcake shops, and you can even make it from a boxed mix. The deep crimson color, which comes from the mixture of red food coloring and cocoa powder, is like a surprise revealed only once the cake is sliced.

You have to trust me when I tell you that the contemporary, butter-free version of red velvet is a winner. No one will know that this cake contains puréed beets, which add sweetness, a gentle color, and loads of moisture. The Norwegian Spiced Chocolate Cake is understated, with just the right amount of sweet and spice.

opposite: Classic Red Velvet Cake

Classic Red Velvet Cake

Makes 12 servings

This a basic butter cake—with cocoa powder for a great chocolate flavor and a bright color that gives it knockout appeal.

FOR THE CAKE
2 tablespoons butter (for the pans)
¼ cup all-purpose flour (for the pans)
2½ cups cake flour
2 tablespoons unsweetened cocoa powder
1 teaspoon baking soda
1 teaspoon kosher or sea salt
2 sticks butter, cubed, at room temperature
2 cups granulated sugar
5 large eggs
1 cup buttermilk
1 teaspoon vanilla extract
1 teaspoon distilled white vinegar
2½ tablespoons red food coloring

FOR THE FROSTING
1 pound cream cheese
2 sticks unsalted butter, at room temperature
1 teaspoon vanilla extract
3 cups powdered sugar

1 For the cake: Preheat the oven to 350°. Butter two 9-inch cake pans (1 tablespoon each), then add 2 tablespoons of the all-purpose flour to each pan. Shake the pans around until they are well dusted (knock out the excess flour and discard) and set aside.
2 Mix the cake flour, cocoa powder, baking soda, and salt together in a large bowl and set aside.
3 Using a hand or stand mixer on medium-low speed, cream the butter and sugar together until pale yellow and uniform. Add the eggs one at a time, beating for about 1 minute after each addition,

until the mixture is uniform. Scrape down the sides of the bowl and beat again. Add the buttermilk, vanilla, vinegar, and food coloring and beat at a low speed, increasing to medium, until smooth. Scrape down the sides of the bowl and beat once more for only a moment, until everything is evenly incorporated.

4 Add a third of the flour mixture to the butter/egg mixture and mix on medium speed until incorporated, then scrape down the sides of the bowl and mix again. Continue this way, adding a third of the flour mixture, scraping down the sides of the bowl between additions, until all the flour is incorporated and the cake batter is smooth.

5 Divide the batter evenly between the two prepared cake pans. Bake until a wooden skewer or toothpick comes out clean when inserted into the center of the cakes, about 30–35 minutes. Remove from the oven and allow the cakes to rest in their pans at least an hour, or until they are completely cool to the touch.

6 For the frosting: Using a hand or stand mixer, beat the cream cheese, butter, and vanilla together until smooth. Add the powdered sugar a cup at a time, beating after each addition (begin at low speed and work up to medium), until all the sugar is added and the frosting is smooth.

7 Frosting the cake: Once the cakes are cool to the touch, remove them from the pans and slice each cake in half horizontally so that you have a total of four "layers." Place one layer, top-side-down, on a cake stand (or a very large dinner plate that can hold the first cake layer flat). Dollop roughly a sixth of the frosting in the middle of the bottom layer and use a small rubber spatula, sandwich spreader, or butter knife to spread the frosting out toward the edges of the cake. Place the second layer, bottom-side-up, on top and repeat with a sixth of the frosting. Continue this way with the two remaining layers, placing the final layer top-side-up; you'll have a third of the frosting left to frost the sides of the cake. Frost the sides of the cake and serve.

Butter-Free Red Velvet Cake

Makes 12 servings

This cake gets its gentle red hue from roasted, puréed beets. Don't be put off by beets! Even if you are not normally a fan of them, they are undetectable in this recipe. They simply add a delicate sweetness and so much moisture to the batter.

Coconut oil replaces butter, and while it's still a fat, it's cholesterol-free.

FOR THE CAKE

2 tablespoons coconut oil (for the pans)

¼ cup all-purpose flour (for the pans)

1 cup buttermilk

1 teaspoon vanilla extract

2 tablespoons unsweetened cocoa powder

1 teaspoon distilled white vinegar

2 medium beets, roasted, peeled, and cut into chunks (about 1 cup)

2½ cups cake flour

1 teaspoon baking soda

1 teaspoon kosher or sea salt

1 cup solid coconut oil

2 cups granulated sugar

5 large eggs

HOW TO ROAST BEETS

Preheat the oven to 400°. Wrap all the beets together in one big piece of aluminum foil, so that there is ½ inch of space between each beet—they shouldn't be squished close together. Place them on a jelly roll pan or in a cast-iron skillet. Place them in the oven and roast for about an hour, or until they are soft and easily pierced with a knife. Remove them from the oven, open the foil, and allow them to cool completely before peeling them with a knife or simply rubbing the skins off using a paper towel (the skins slip off easily).

FOR THE FROSTING

1 pound cream cheese
½ cup solid coconut oil
1 teaspoon vanilla extract
3 cups powdered sugar

1 For the cake: Preheat the oven to 350°. Smear the coconut oil on two 9-inch cake pans (1 tablespoon each), then add 2 tablespoons of the flour to each pan. Shake the pans around until they are well dusted (knock out the excess flour and discard) and set aside.

2 Place the buttermilk, vanilla, cocoa powder, vinegar, and beets in the bowl of a food processor (or use a blender). Process for 20 seconds, scrape down the sides of the bowl, and process again for 20 seconds more, or until smooth. Set aside.

3 Mix the cake flour, baking soda, and salt together in a large bowl and set aside.

4 Using a hand or stand mixer at medium-low speed, cream the solid coconut oil and sugar together until uniform. Add the eggs one at a time, beating after each addition until the mixture is uniform. Scrape down the sides of the bowl and beat again. Add the buttermilk/beet mixture and beat on low speed, increasing to medium, until smooth. Scrape down the sides of the bowl and beat once more for only a moment, until everything is evenly incorporated.

5 Add a third of the cake flour mixture to the wet mixture and mix on medium speed until incorporated, then scrape down the sides of the bowl and mix again. Continue this way, adding a third of the flour mixture at a time and scraping down the sides of the bowl after each addition, until all of the flour is incorporated and the cake batter is smooth.

6 Divide the batter evenly between the two prepared cake pans. Bake until a wooden skewer or toothpick comes out clean when inserted into the center of the cakes, about 30–35 minutes. Remove from the oven and allow the cakes to rest in their pans for at least an hour, or until they are completely cool to the touch.

7 For the frosting: Using a hand or stand mixer set on medium speed, beat the cream cheese, coconut oil, and vanilla until smooth. Add the powdered sugar a cup at a time, beating after each addition (begin at low speed and work up to medium), until all the sugar is added and the frosting is smooth.

8 Frosting the cake: Once the cakes are cool to the touch, remove them from the pans and slice each cake in half horizontally so that you have a total of four "layers." Place one layer, top-side-down, on a cake stand (or a very large dinner plate that can hold the first cake layer flat). Dollop roughly a sixth of the frosting in the middle of the bottom layer and use a small rubber spatula, sand-wich spreader, or butter knife to spread the frosting out toward the edges of the cake. Place the second layer, bottom-side-up, on top and repeat with a sixth of the frosting. Continue this way with the two remaining layers, placing the final layer top-side-up; you'll have a third of the frosting left to frost the sides of the cake. Frost the sides of the cake and serve.

Norwegian Spiced Chocolate Cake

This lovely cake, known in Norway as Tropisk Aroma, is equally balanced between sweet, chocolate, and spice—no one flavor overwhelms the cake. While it feels very grown-up, children love it too. This cake is baked in a Bundt cake pan, not because that is typical of the classic Norwegian recipe but because it's fun.

Makes 12 servings

FOR THE CAKE
1 tablespoon butter (for the pan)
¼ cup all-purpose flour (for the pan)
2½ cups cake flour
2 tablespoons unsweetened cocoa powder
1 teaspoon baking soda
1 teaspoon ground nutmeg
1½ teaspoons cinnamon
2 sticks butter, cubed, at room temperature
2 cups granulated sugar
5 large eggs
1 cup buttermilk
1 teaspoon vanilla extract

FOR THE GLAZE

1 teaspoon instant, decaffeinated coffee grounds
2 tablespoons boiling water
1 ounce (1 square) unsweetened baking chocolate
1 tablespoon butter
Pinch of kosher or sea salt
1 cup powdered sugar

1 For the cake: Preheat the oven to 325°. Butter a 12-inch Bundt cake pan, then shake the all-purpose flour around the pan until it's well dusted (knock out the excess flour and discard) and set aside.

2 Mix the cake flour, cocoa powder, baking soda, nutmeg, and cinnamon together in a large bowl and set aside. Using a hand or stand mixer on medium-low speed, cream the butter and sugar together until pale yellow and uniform. Add the eggs one at a time, beating after each addition until the mixture is uniform. Scrape down the sides of the bowl and beat again. Add the buttermilk and vanilla and beat on low speed, increasing to medium, until smooth. Scrape down the sides of the bowl and beat once more for only a moment, until everything is evenly incorporated.

3 Add a third of the flour mixture to the butter/egg mixture and mix at medium speed until incorporated, then scrape down the sides of the bowl and mix again. Continue this way, adding a third of the flour at a time, scraping down the bowl after each addition, until all of the flour is incorporated and the batter is smooth.

4 Pour the batter into the prepared pan. Bake until a wooden skewer or toothpick comes out clean when inserted into the center of the cake, about 50–60 minutes. Remove from the oven and allow the cake to rest in its pan until completely cool, at least 90 minutes.

5 Turn the cake pan over onto a flat surface (like a cutting board) and tap the bottom of the pan; the cake should slide out smoothly.

6 For the glaze: Stir the instant coffee grounds and boiling water together in a cup and set aside. In a microwave-safe bowl, microwave the chocolate and butter together at full power for 15 seconds, stir well, and microwave again for 15 seconds. Keep this pattern up, microwaving for 15-second intervals and stirring well after each, as residual heat from the chocolate will help melt the mixture. The mixture should be just melted. Make sure not to overheat it; you'll know if it's overheated because it will smell burnt.

7 Add the coffee and salt to the chocolate and stir to combine. Add the powdered sugar a little at a time, beating it in with a wire whisk or fork until a smooth pourable glaze forms. If it gets too thick, add 1 teaspoon of hot water at a time until it's of pouring consistency. Drizzle it over the cooled cake and serve.

Classic Pecan Pie

CONTEMPORARY **CRISPY MINI PECAN TARTS**

INTERNATIONAL **MEXICAN CHOCOLATE PECAN PIE**

Unapologetically sweet, pecan pie is a mainstay on southern tables. Pecan trees are prolific in southern states. During pecan season, a neighbor, friend, or friend-of-a-friend will inevitably (and fortunately) offer me unshelled pecans from trees on their land. The pecan trees meander a bit into the Midwest, but Georgia is the largest producer of these nuts, which may be why southerners proclaim pecan pie to be a southern dessert.

Old-school corn syrup and brown sugar lie behind the pie's intense sweetness. Because of this, the crust doesn't need much sugar; it and the rich nuts play well off of the sweet filling. While corn syrup is used in the Classic and International versions, you'll notice that I've replaced it with maple syrup in the Crispy Mini Pecan Tarts recipe. Maple syrup is a sort of natural version of corn syrup, and I find that it can be used interchangeably in many recipes.

Mexican Chocolate Pecan Pie is rich, and its depth of flavor is due in equal parts to the chocolate and the cinnamon—two ingredients integral to Mexican cooking.

opposite: Classic Pecan Pie

Classic Pecan Pie

Makes one 9-inch pie

Although pecan pie is a mainstay on many holiday tables across the country, it wasn't really a known dessert until the twentieth century. Karo Syrup (a corn syrup manufacturer) claims that one of its sales executives' wives invented the pie in the 1930s, forever changing the American Thanksgiving dessert menu. Because the pie filling is egg-based, it should jiggle a bit when pulled from the oven—a slight jiggle doesn't mean it's not fully baked.

1 cup pecan pieces

1 cup pecan halves (to decorate top of pie)

1 disk homemade pie dough (page 98 [omit cheese] and page 99 [steps 1–3])

2 cups dried beans or uncooked rice (for baking the crust)

1 cup lightly packed light brown sugar

½ teaspoon kosher or sea salt

¾ cup light corn syrup

1 teaspoon vanilla extract

5 tablespoons butter, melted and cooled to room temperature

3 eggs

2 teaspoons bourbon

The key to light, flaky piecrust is using very cold fat (butter and shortening or lard) and being careful not to overwork (overmix) the dough. This is equally true for dessert pies and savory pies.

1 Preheat the oven to 350°. Arrange the pecans (both pieces and halves) in a single layer on a jelly roll pan, keeping the pieces and halves separate from each other, and bake until fragrant, 5–7 minutes. As soon as you can smell them, take them out of the oven and immediately transfer to a dinner plate to stop the baking process. (Because of their dense oil content, nuts can go from nicely toasted to burnt very quickly and will continue to cook even after they are out of the oven.) Set aside.

2 Increase the oven temperature to 400°. Remove the pie dough from the refrigerator 10 minutes before rolling.

3 Lightly flour a clean work surface and roll the dough into a 12-inch round about ¼ inch thick. Fold the dough loosely in half to transfer it to an ungreased 9-inch pie pan; with the seam in the middle, unfold the dough so that it covers the dish. Lightly press the dough against the sides and bottom of the pan, being careful not to stretch it. Fold any excess dough hanging over the rim of the pan up under itself and crimp the edges.

4 Lay a sheet of parchment paper or foil on top of the pie dough and push it down to fit the shape of the dish. Pour in the dried beans or uncooked rice, making sure they fill the dish evenly.

5 Bake for 15 minutes, then lift out the parchment paper or foil with the beans/rice (they can be composted or used again) and bake for 10 minutes longer. Remove the pie shell from the oven and turn the heat down to 350°.

6 Whisk together the brown sugar, salt, corn syrup, vanilla, butter, eggs, and bourbon until smooth. Add just the pecan pieces and stir until well incorporated. Pour this mixture into the pie shell and lay the pecan halves on top (frustratingly, some will sink, but that's okay). Carefully put the pie in the oven and bake for 30 minutes. Remove the pie from the oven, and cover it loosely with a sheet of foil so the crust doesn't burn. Continue to bake for 30–40 minutes longer, or until the center is just set, with a slight jiggle. Allow to cool at room temperature for at least 2 hours before serving.

Crispy Mini Pecan Tarts

🍴

Makes 15 tarts

These bite-sized pecan tarts pack a big crunch because of the crisp filo cups. They are great to bring to a potluck (easily sharable) and are also the perfect size when you want just a few bites of dessert.

1 package mini filo cups (15 count, found in the freezer section of most grocery stores)
¾ cup chopped pecans
½ cup maple syrup
1 egg
1 tablespoon melted coconut oil
1 tablespoon lightly packed light brown sugar
1 teaspoon bourbon
¼ teaspoon kosher or sea salt

1 Remove the filo cups from the freezer and set aside. Preheat the oven to 350°. Arrange the pecans in a single layer on a jelly roll pan and bake until fragrant, 5–7 minutes. As soon as you can smell them, take them out of the oven and immediately transfer to a dinner plate. (Because of their dense oil content, nuts can go from nicely toasted to burnt very quickly and will continue to cook even after they are out of the oven.) Set aside.

2 In a large bowl, using a wire whisk or table fork, beat the maple syrup, egg, coconut oil, brown sugar, bourbon, and salt until smooth. Set aside.

3 Once the pecans have cooled completely, evenly distribute them between the mini filo cups (the cups will still be cold, which is fine). Using a teaspoon, fill each cup three-quarters full with the filling (you may have a bit left over). Don't be tempted to overfill them, as this will cause the filling to bubble over and burn. Bake for 15 minutes. They will smell wonderfully nutty and sweet, and the filo shells will be crisp and slightly golden. Remove from the oven and allow to cool 30 minutes before serving.

Crispy Mini Pecan Tarts

Mexican Chocolate Pecan Pie

Makes one 9-inch pie

Cinnamon and chocolate go together hand in hand and add a delicious flavor element to this pie. Make sure to use bittersweet chocolate, as called for; it adds a depth without adding too much sugar.

FOR THE CRUST
12 plain graham cracker sheets, crushed
   (about 2 cups crumbs)
1 teaspoon cinnamon
¼ teaspoon kosher or sea salt
¼ cup packed light brown sugar
1 stick butter, melted

FOR THE FILLING
1 cup pecan pieces
1 cup pecan halves
¾ cup packed light brown sugar
½ teaspoon kosher or sea salt
¾ cup light corn syrup
1 teaspoon vanilla extract

5 tablespoons butter, melted and cooled

3 eggs, whisked

2 teaspoons bourbon

3 ounces bittersweet chocolate, grated (about 1 cup)

1 For the crust: Generously spray a 9-inch pie plate with nonstick cooking spray. In a small bowl, stir together the graham cracker crumbs, cinnamon, salt, brown sugar, and butter until they are evenly combined and press them into the pie plate, first with your hands and then using the bottom of a juice glass, making sure that the thickness is even on the bottom and sides of the pan. Refrigerate for at least 30 minutes (up to 24 hours).

2 For the filling: Preheat the oven to 350°. Arrange the pecans on a jelly roll pan, keeping the pieces and halves separate from each other. Bake for 5–7 minutes—you will be able to smell them when they are toasted. Remove them from the oven and immediately transfer them to a plate. (Because of their dense oil content, nuts can go from nicely toasted to burnt very quickly and will continue to cook even after they are out of the oven.)

3 In a large bowl, using a wire whisk, beat the sugar, salt, corn syrup, vanilla, butter, eggs, bourbon, and chocolate until smooth. Add just the pecan pieces and stir well to combine. Pour the filling into the pie shell and arrange the pecan halves on top in a pretty design (frustratingly, some will sink, but that's okay). Carefully place the pie in the oven and bake for 30 minutes; cover the pie loosely with a sheet of foil so the crust doesn't burn and continue to bake for 30–40 minutes longer, or until the center is just set. Allow to cool at room temperature for at least 2 hours before serving.

24

Classic Coconut Cake

CONTEMPORARY COCONUT CAKE WITH BROWN SUGAR FROSTING

INTERNATIONAL JAMAICAN COCONUT SPICE CAKE

I know a number of southerners who will generously share any of their family recipes except one: coconut cake. A good coconut cake recipe is like a cherished antique handed down from generation to generation—it's to be admired and enjoyed by many, but handled only by very few. Coconut cake, like the red velvet cake, is a butter cake (similar to a pound cake, in that butter is a main ingredient) with layers of shredded coconut and coconut flavors. If you can make a basic butter cake, you can make dozens of variations simply by changing the flavoring ingredients.

Developing the Coconut Cake with Brown Sugar Frosting changed the way I make coconut cake altogether. The frosting is so light and silky, and it's hard to believe there is no fat in it at all. The Jamaican Coconut Spice Cake doesn't call for too much sugar and has no frosting, making it a perfect snack any time of day.

opposite: Classic Coconut Cake

Classic Coconut Cake

Makes 12 servings

Creamy, rich, decadent—this is a cake worthy of celebration. Seeing a homemade coconut cake on a sideboard or beneath a cake dome signals that a fabulous meal lies ahead. Many layers of coconut flavor infuse this cake. I replaced dairy milk with unsweetened coconut milk, and then the cake batter also features coconut extract and shredded coconut.

FOR THE CAKE
2 tablespoons unsalted butter (for the pans)
¼ cup all-purpose flour (for the pans)
3 cups cake flour (plus ¼ cup for the pans)
1 teaspoon kosher or sea salt
1 tablespoon baking powder
1½ cups sweetened shredded coconut
2 sticks unsalted butter, cubed, at room temperature
1¾ cups granulated sugar
5 large eggs
1 teaspoon coconut extract
1 teaspoon vanilla extract
1 cup coconut milk (shake can well before opening)

FOR THE FROSTING
1 pound cream cheese
2 sticks unsalted butter, at room temperature
1 teaspoon coconut extract
1 teaspoon vanilla extract
3 cups powdered sugar
2 cups sweetened shredded coconut

1 For the cake: Preheat the oven to 350°. Butter two 9-inch cake pans (1 tablespoon each), then add 2 tablespoons of the all-purpose flour to each pan. Shake the pans around until they are well dusted (knock out the excess flour and discard) and set aside.

2 Mix the cake flour, salt, baking powder, and coconut together in a large bowl and set aside.

3 Using a hand or stand mixer on medium-low speed, cream the butter and sugar together until pale yellow and uniform. Add the eggs one at a time, beating for about 1 minute after each addition, until the batter is uniform. Scrape down the sides of the bowl and beat again. Add the coconut extract, vanilla extract, and coconut milk and beat on low speed, increasing to medium, until smooth. Scrape down the sides of the bowl and beat once more just until everything is evenly incorporated.

4 Add a third of the flour mixture to the butter/egg mixture and mix on medium speed until incorporated, then scrape down the sides of the bowl and mix again. Continue this way, adding a third of the flour mixture at a time, scraping down the sides of the bowl after each addition, until all the flour is incorporated and the batter is smooth.

5 Divide the batter evenly between the two prepared cake pans (about 3 cups of batter per pan). Bake until a wooden skewer or toothpick comes out clean when inserted into the center of the cakes, about 30 minutes. Remove from the oven and allow the cakes to rest in their pans for at least an hour, or until completely cool to the touch.

6 For the frosting: Using a hand or stand mixer, beat the cream cheese, butter, coconut extract, and vanilla extract together until smooth. Add the powdered sugar a cup at a time, beating after each addition (begin at low speed and work up to medium), until all the sugar is added and the frosting is smooth.

7 Frosting the cake: Once the cakes are cool to the touch, remove them from the pans and slice each cake in half horizontally so that you have a total of four "layers." Place one layer, top-side-down, on a cake stand (or a very large dinner plate that can hold the first cake layer flat). Dollop roughly a sixth of the frosting in the middle of the bottom layer and use a small rubber spatula, sandwich spreader, or butter knife to spread the frosting out toward the edges of the cake. Place the second layer, bottom-side-up, on top and repeat with a sixth of the frosting. Continue this way with the two remaining layers, placing the final layer top-side-up; you'll have a third of the frosting left to frost the sides of the cake. Frost the sides of the cake, then scatter the shredded coconut over the top of the cake and press it into the sides. Serve.

Coconut Cake with Brown Sugar Frosting

Makes 12–16 servings

"Layers of flavor"—that's a phrase I use all the time. As I tell my students and viewers, you have to layer flavors, one on top of another, to create really great-tasting foods. Nowhere is layering flavors more evident than in this cake. The cake has shredded coconut, coconut oil, and a dash of coconut extract, while the frosting is made from whipped egg whites and brown sugar, creating a super-light, marshmallow-like effect.

This cake is great for a crowd because it's made in a baking dish and frosted right in the pan (it's a "sheet cake," not a layer cake). It's not as fancy as a layer cake, but absolutely mouthwatering. As soon as I developed the frosting recipe, I knew that I would use it on more than just coconut cakes. It's much lighter than butter-based frostings and uses less sugar. It's a fabulous finish to a delicious cake.

PEAK STAGES

The longer and/or harder you whip egg whites, the more air is incorporated into them, and the firmer and stiffer they become. Most recipes will indicate how firm your whipped egg whites need to be by referring to the following stages:

No peaks: Egg whites are frothy and uniform but still very liquid—they can't hold any shape at all.

Soft peaks: Peaks can hold for a moment but quickly fold entirely back on themselves.

Firm peaks: Peaks hold up, but the tips of the peaks fold back on themselves.

Stiff peaks: Peaks hold their shape strongly, without folding.

FOR THE CAKE

3 cups cake flour
1 teaspoon kosher or sea salt
1 tablespoon baking powder
1½ cups sweetened shredded coconut
1 cup solid coconut oil
1¾ cups granulated sugar
5 large eggs
1 teaspoon coconut extract
1 teaspoon vanilla extract
1 cup coconut milk (shake the can well before opening)

FOR THE FROSTING

4 egg whites, at room temperature
⅔ cup lightly packed light brown sugar
Pinch of kosher or sea salt
½ teaspoon cream of tartar
½ teaspoon vanilla extract
½ teaspoon coconut extract
1½ cups sweetened shredded coconut

Coconut Cake with Brown Sugar Frosting

1 For the cake: Preheat the oven to 350°. Generously spray a
   9 × 11-inch baking dish with nonstick cooking spray and set aside.

2 Mix the cake flour, salt, baking powder, and shredded coconut
   together in a large bowl and set aside. Using a hand or stand
   mixer on medium-low speed, cream the coconut oil and sugar
   together until fluffy (it will not "cream" the way butter and sugar
   do). Add the eggs one at a time, beating after each addition until
   the batter is uniform. Scrape down the sides of the bowl and
   beat again. Add the coconut extract, vanilla extract, and coconut
   milk and beat on low speed, increasing to medium, until smooth.
   Scrape down the sides of the bowl and beat once more for only
   a moment, until everything is evenly incorporated.

3 Add a third of the flour mixture to the coconut oil/egg mixture
   and mix on medium speed until incorporated, then scrape down
   the sides of the bowl and mix again. Continue this way, adding a
   third of the flour mixture at a time, scraping down the sides of the
   bowl after each addition, until all of the flour has been incorporated and the batter is smooth.

4 Pour the batter into the prepared baking dish and bake for
   35–45 minutes, or until a toothpick inserted in the center comes
   out clean. Remove from the oven and allow the cake to rest in the
   dish for at least an hour, until completely cool to the touch.

5 For the frosting: Fill a 2- or 3-quart saucepan halfway with hot
   water. Place a large, heat-proof mixing bowl (stainless steel is
   ideal, but heat-resistant glass, like Pyrex brand, is fine; just don't
   use plastic) on top of the saucepan. Make sure the mixing bowl
   fits snugly and the bottom does not touch the water. Remove
   the bowl, turn the burner to high, and bring the water to a boil.
   As soon as it comes to a boil, turn the heat down to medium-low
   so that the water is just gently simmering.

6 Meanwhile, in the mixing bowl, use a balloon whisk to whisk together the egg whites, sugar, and salt just to combine. Have a stand or hand mixer set up and ready to go.

7 Place the mixing bowl with the egg mixture over the simmering water and whisk vigorously for 1 minute. Don't stop whisking—if you do, the eggs could become a sugary omelet. You are gently melting the sugar. Quickly add the cream of tartar and whisk constantly for 2 minutes more, or until the sugar has melted and the mixture is very hot, looks glossy, and has reached the soft peak stage.

8 Remove the mixing bowl from the simmering water, add the vanilla extract and coconut extract, and, using your mixer, continue whipping the mixture, starting on low speed and gradually increasing to medium-high, until firm peaks form, about 3–4 minutes.

9 Frosting the cake: Dollop all of the frosting onto the middle of the completely cooled cake. Push the frosting out to the corners using a sandwich spreader or butter knife. Sprinkle evenly with shredded coconut and serve. Store any leftover cake in the refrigerator.

Jamaican Coconut Spice Cake

Makes 12–16 servings

The wonderful spicy scent of this cake will fill your kitchen as it bakes. It's a traditional Jamaican cake with one addition, sour cream, which makes it super-moist. This is not so much a sugary-sweet dessert cake— it's more of a snack cake. It goes great with a cup of coffee and is also a nice treat in a child's lunchbox.

3 cups all-purpose flour
2 teaspoons baking powder
1 teaspoon baking soda
½ teaspoon allspice
½ teaspoon nutmeg
½ teaspoon cinnamon
1 teaspoon kosher or sea salt
2 cups sweetened shredded coconut
1 stick butter, cubed, at room temperature
1 cup granulated sugar
1 cup sour cream
2 eggs
1 teaspoon vanilla
1 cup milk

1 Preheat the oven to 375°. Spray a 9 × 11-inch baking dish with nonstick cooking spray and set aside.

2 In a large bowl, mix together the flour, baking powder, baking soda, allspice, nutmeg, cinnamon, salt, and coconut. Set aside.

3 In a stand mixer, or using a hand mixer, cream the butter and sugar together until uniform and pale yellow. Mix for 1 minute on medium-low, then scrape down the sides of the bowl and mix on medium-low for another minute. Scrape down the sides of the bowl again and add the sour cream. Mix for 30 seconds, scrape down the sides of the bowl, and add the eggs and the vanilla. Mix until completely combined, scrape down the sides of the bowl, and add the milk. Mix until smooth.

4 Add a third of the flour mixture to the butter/sour cream/egg mixture and mix on medium speed until incorporated, then scrape down the sides of the bowl and mix again. Continue this way, adding a third of the flour mixture at a time, scraping down the sides of the bowl after each addition, until the flour is incorporated and the batter is smooth.

5 Pour the batter into the prepared baking dish and bake for 30 minutes. The cake will be a rich brown color and smell spicy and amazing. Remove from the oven and allow to cool in the pan for 30 minutes, then cut into squares.

Classic Fruit Cobbler

CONTEMPORARY **SAVORY VEGETABLE COBBLER WITH QUINOA CRUST**

INTERNATIONAL **DUTCH APPLE BABY**

Cobblers are traditionally made with fruit topped by a batter, biscuit, or piecrust. They can be savory, too (as you will see in the Savory Vegetable Cobbler with Quinoa Crust). Southern cobblers are traditionally made using one fruit, like raspberry or blackberry, but can also feature a combination. The cobbler has culinary cousins all over the United States and the United Kingdom. Similar recipes have names like Betty, dump, slump, grump, buckle, and, in North Carolina, sonker. Just hearing any of these names makes me think we are in for a fun dessert.

Anytime I can make a recipe that involves spinach, artichoke hearts, and Parmesan, I am all over it, which is why I especially love this vegetable cobbler with a quinoa crust. Use Parmigiano-Reggiano for this recipe if possible. The Dutch Apple Baby is like a giant, delicious pancake that has a real wow factor and is beautiful served straight from the oven.

Classic Fruit Cobbler

Makes 8 servings

While this dessert is wonderful—warm, straight out of the oven— any time of year, it's best in the summer, when local fruits are plentiful, ripe, and juicy.

You'll notice that the fruit is macerated before baking, which means that it soaks in the juices that are coaxed from the fruit by the use of sugar. This step softens the fruit.

Piling the macerated fruit on top of the batter rather than the other way around makes the finished dish look more interesting—craggy and imperfect, with bits of fruit popping through in spots. Berries work well in this recipe, and so do stone fruits such as peaches, nectarines, or even plums. If you're using berries, leave them whole, but if you're using stone fruits, remove the stones (or pits) and slice the fruit into thin pieces.

1 tablespoon butter (for the pan)
3 cups ripe fruit
⅛ teaspoon cinnamon
2 teaspoons lightly packed light brown sugar
1 cup all-purpose flour
1 cup granulated sugar
½ teaspoon kosher or sea salt
2½ teaspoons baking powder
1 cup milk
1 stick unsalted butter, melted
¼ teaspoon vanilla extract

1. Preheat the oven to 375°. Grease a 9 × 11-inch baking dish with the butter and set aside. Place the fruit in a bowl and toss it with the cinnamon and brown sugar.

2. In a separate large bowl, combine the flour, granulated sugar, salt, and baking powder; stir well to combine. Add the milk, butter, and vanilla and use a wire whisk to mix until just smooth. Pour the batter into the prepared baking dish, smoothing out the top with a rubber spatula.

3. Arrange the fruit evenly over the top of the batter. Bake for 45–55 minutes, or until crust pops up over the fruit and is light golden. Remove from the oven and allow to rest for 5 minutes, then serve (with vanilla ice cream, if you like).

Classic Fruit Cobbler

Savory Vegetable Cobbler with Quinoa Crust

Makes 8 servings

In this recipe the classic cobbler is transformed into a delicious vegetarian main dish or side dish; it's so scrumptious that omnivores will love it too. Tomatoes, fresh spinach, and artichoke hearts are beautifully complemented by tarragon. Adding Parmesan to the quinoa crust provides another layer of savory flavor. Don't look for the crust to pop up over the veggies, as it does in the Classic Fruit Cobbler. It will remain beneath the vegetables, soaking up all that flavor.

Quinoa is a seed, indigenous to South America. It's high in protein and gluten free. It's very important to cook quinoa in a flavorful liquid, even if that flavor is only salted water. Vegetable, chicken, or beef broth works well, too. Allow time (15 minutes) to soak the quinoa before cooking—this is an important step, not to be skipped.

¾ cup quinoa

1 cup flavorful liquid (like vegetable, chicken, or beef broth)

1 tablespoon solid coconut oil plus ⅓ cup melted

2 medium tomatoes, seeds removed, chopped (about 2 cups)

3 cups (packed) fresh baby spinach

1 teaspoon kosher or sea salt

3 green onions (including dark green tops) or
⅓ yellow onion, chopped

2 teaspoons chopped fresh tarragon (or ½ teaspoon dried)

1 (15-ounce) can artichoke heart quarters, drained and
squeezed as dry as possible

1 cup all-purpose flour

1 cup freshly grated Parmesan cheese

2½ teaspoons baking powder

1 cup milk

1 Place the quinoa in a bowl and cover with water by 1 inch. Soak for 15 minutes. Drain well in a mesh sieve. Transfer the quinoa to a small pot and add the flavorful liquid. Set over medium-high heat.

2 Watch closely, and as soon as steam comes out of the pot and the liquid is simmering strongly, cover the pot, reduce the heat to the lowest setting, and allow the quinoa to cook very gently until all the liquid is absorbed, about 15–25 minutes.

3 Preheat the oven to 375°. Grease a 9 × 11-inch baking dish with the solid coconut oil; set aside.

4 Toss the tomatoes and spinach with the salt in a large bowl. Allow to sit for 30 minutes (this is a different way to macerate; the salt will draw out much of the vegetables' liquid). After 30 minutes, squeeze as much of the liquid out of the vegetables as possible and return them to the bowl. (You can drink the naturally yummy vegetable juice or discard it.)

5 Add the onions, tarragon, and artichokes and toss to combine.

6 In a separate large bowl, using a wire whisk, mix together the flour, quinoa, Parmesan, and baking powder, then stir in the milk and melted coconut oil, until a consistent batter forms.

7 Pour the batter into the prepared baking dish and arrange the vegetables evenly over the top. Bake for 45–55 minutes, or until the crust is golden and cooked through. Remove from the oven and allow to rest for 5 minutes before serving.

Dutch Apple Baby

Makes 2 main-course servings or 4 side-dish servings

The story goes that the Dutch Apple Baby was created by German immigrants in a Seattle, Washington, restaurant around 1900. Light and airy, with crisp edges, the Dutch Apple Baby is a modified German pancake and makes an impressive breakfast or brunch dish. It's similar to a cobbler because of the batter, but different because it includes eggs and is baked in a preheated skillet rather than a baking dish. Keep in mind that as soon as the Dutch Apple Baby hits room temperature, its gorgeous, crisp sides will begin to fall, so serve it straight from the oven.

2 medium-sized tart apples (like Granny Smith), cored and
    each cut into 24 slices (about 3 cups)
⅓ cup packed light brown sugar
½ teaspoon ground cinnamon
½ teaspoon ground ginger
¼ teaspoon ground nutmeg
4 tablespoons butter, divided
¾ cup all-purpose flour
½ teaspoon kosher or sea salt
½ teaspoon baking powder

1 cup milk
1 teaspoon vanilla extract
4 eggs
1 tablespoon granulated sugar
Powdered sugar for dusting

1 Preheat the oven to 425°. In a large bowl, toss the apples with the brown sugar, cinnamon, ginger, and nutmeg and set aside.

2 Place a nonstick skillet over medium-high heat and add 2 table-spoons of the butter. The butter will froth, then the frothing will subside. Add the apple slices. Stir, cover, and cook for 2 minutes, or until the sugar melts and bubbles, then uncover and reduce the heat to medium-low or low so that the apples cook gently. Continue cooking for about 3–4 minutes, stirring occasionally, until the apples are soft and their skin color fades.

3 Meanwhile, place a 10-inch cast-iron skillet or heavy sauté pan in the oven; getting the skillet hot this way will help make the Baby crispy.

4 In a small bowl, stir together the flour, salt, and baking powder. In a large bowl use a wire whisk to mix together the milk, vanilla, eggs, and granulated sugar. Whisk the dry ingredients (flour, salt, baking powder) into the wet ingredients (milk, vanilla, eggs, sugar) until smooth.

5 Using sturdy oven mitts, carefully remove the hot skillet from the oven and place it on a heat-resistant work space (like your stove top). Immediately add the remaining butter and swirl it around to coat the pan. As soon as the butter melts, pour in the batter and then carefully arrange the cooked apples in the middle. There should be a least an inch of batter exposed around the edge of the pan so that the Dutch Baby can rise.

6 Immediately transfer the pan to the oven and bake for 20–25 minutes, or until the sides have risen and are golden and crisp. The middle should be creamy and custard-like. Shake powdered sugar over the top and serve immediately.

Dutch Apple Baby

Index